OP 7⁵⁴⁄

COUNTRY
ARCHITECTURE

COUNTRY ARCHITECTURE

Old-Fashioned Designs for
Gazebos, Summerhouses, Springhouses,
Smokehouses, Stables, Greenhouses,
Carriage Houses, Outhouses, Icehouses,
Barns, Doghouses, Sheds, and Other
Outbuildings

Lawrence Grow

The Main Street Press
Pittstown, New Jersey

First edition 1985

All rights reserved

Copyright © 1985 by The Main Street Press

Published by
The Main Street Press, Inc.
William Case House
Pittstown, NJ 08867

Published simultaneously in Canada by
Methuen Publications
2330 Midland Avenue
Agincourt, Ontario M1S 1P7

Printed in the United States of America

Designed by Lisa Magaz

Library of Congress Cataloging-in-Publication Data

Grow, Lawrence.
    Country architecture.

    Bibliography: p.
    1. Outbuildings—United States. 2. Outbuildings—
United States—Designs and plans. I. Title.
NA8301.G76 1985   728′.9′0973   85-24026
ISBN 0-915590-80-8 (pbk.)

Contents

Introduction

The wonderful variety of buildings found in rural North America is a source of much delight to European travelers and commentators. Continually presented at home with a view of a synthetic, disposable society through films and television, these visitors are surprised to find the past so alive in our small villages and along secluded back roads. As we do so many things in the New World, we tend to take our country architectural heritage for granted, giving it little thought and even less care. We are so busy traveling at a fast rate from one city to another that we often simply do not see the richness of the manmade landscape which still remains. Numbed perhaps by the sameness of modern urban commercial centers from coast to coast, we rarely stop to enjoy the truly picturesque examples of colonial and Victorian rural architecture which have stood the test of time. Let *Country Architecture* be your guide to this remarkable collection of buildings.

Special types of buildings such as springhouses and smokehouses, barns and carriage houses, privies and stables, summer kitchens and woodsheds—to name some of the categories—are the focus of this illustrated book. These are the seemingly expendable buildings, many of which are no longer needed for their original purpose. They are easily neglected, even by country people who should know better. Another volume is planned on the country house, a species less threatened than the outbuildings that surround it.

Thousands of designs for barns and other outbuildings were published in farm journals and books during the 19th century. The improvement of farm buildings was always on the minds of agricultural writers. They were also not unappreciative of aesthetic considerations. Outbuildings, one writer advised in 1882, should "present a neat appearance. They can be pleasing objects, and impart an impression of comfort and completeness upon all who see them. This attractive appearance will depend upon the symmetry and exterior finish of the buildings themselves, their grouping, and planting of suitable shade trees, etc."

Beginning in the 1850s, many architectural writers, including Lewis Allen, Calvert Vaux, and Andrew Jackson Downing, devoted considerable attention to such outbuildings as the stable, the carriage house, various kinds of garden structures, and even as lowly a structure as the privy. In their books these writers were addressing a wealthier and better educated group of country dwellers than the readers of the agricultural press. Country gentlemen were as interested then as they are today in presenting a handsome face to the world.

Nonetheless, there are many more similarities than differences between the properties of the gentleman farmer and his working counterpart. All farms—and, indeed, many village properties—had need of a barn large enough for at least one cow, a horse or two, a wagon, and space sufficient for storing grain, hay, and straw. And every property required a privy, a structure to enclose the spring or hand-dug well, and a storehouse or shed for wood. The inclusion of other buildings such as a smokehouse, summer kitchen, summerhouse or gazebo, icehouse, henhouse, and piggery depended upon either the needs of a particular type of farming operation or the use of the property.

Almost all rural architecture is vernacular, that is, without a marked stylistic character. It is untutored, without a professional architectural imprint. This is particularly true of most surviving examples of colonial-period outbuildings, many of them log structures or primitive fieldstone buildings. For this reason, it is all the more remarkable that outbuildings present such a striking appearance. Farmers, whether of the 18th or the 19th century, seemed to have an almost unerring sense of how to site and raise a building so that it would appear to be a part of the natural landscape and not alien to it. There was, of course, a practical reason for angling a springhouse in to the side of a hillside, thereby gaining an extra measure of free insulation. And a barn located, as one contemporary writer explained, "upon a rise of ground, where a cellar can be built, opening upon the lower ground to the rear," was a useful solution to the problem of stabling on one floor and storing hay and straw on another.

Whether for practical or aesthetic reasons—or a combination of both—farm and country village outbuildings of imaginative design and form were built throughout North America during the colonial and Victorian centuries. They are far superior in almost every way to such counterparts today as the prefabricated aluminum carriage shed or tool house and the cinderblock dairy barn. It is no wonder that many country dwellers will employ a team of Amish or Mennonite farmers from hundreds of miles away to erect a new timber-framed barn. Anyone today with a knowledge of the construction techniques of yesterday and the skill to employ them is blessed with a profession for life.

Country Architecture is intended to bring to light much which is easily forgotten if not lost about rural outbuildings. The hundreds of drawings of building elevations, details, and floor plans are useful and may be copied freely. The material is drawn largely from the archives of the Historic American Buildings Survey of the National Park Service, U.S. Department of the Interior, and is on deposit at the Library of Congress.

1. Carriage Houses and Wagon Sheds

Carriage houses and wagon sheds were once as commonly encountered in the country and suburbs as garages are today. Even in the city, there had to be a place to store the buggy or delivery wagon. Such buildings were commonly set apart from the house and were roomy enough to provide stabling for horses and storage for harnesses and feed. The buildings varied greatly in execution, from the humble open wagon shed used to house farm wagons to elegant quarters for stylish carriages intended only for the transport of people. Most rural and village buildings were of simple wood-frame construction and greatly resembled cow barns, although built on a smaller scale. Ample provision was usually made for turn-around space, and running water was often piped in so that vehicles could be washed down after heavy use. The everyday farmer or mechanic wanted only a utilitarian space and often used it for storing grain or equipment as well. Gentlemen farmers and more affluent suburban and city dwellers frequently built brick, stone, or fanciful wood carriage houses of considerable distinction.

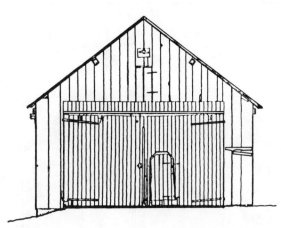

West-southwest elevation, wagon shed, Dundore Farm, Mt. Pleasant vicinity, Pa., c. 1840.

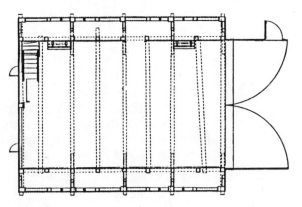

Floor plan.

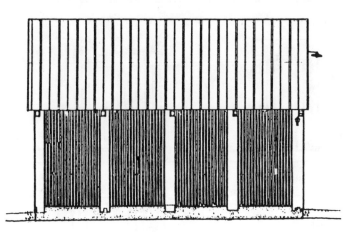

North-northwest elevation.

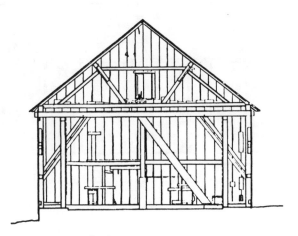

Sectional view.

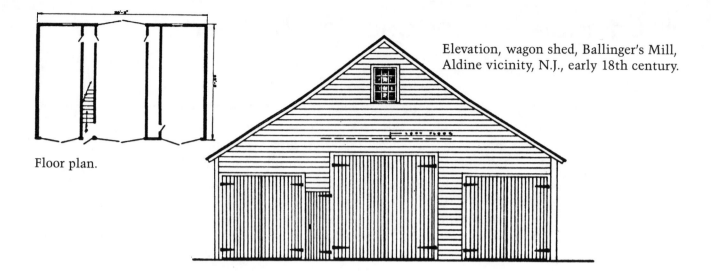

Floor plan.

Elevation, wagon shed, Ballinger's Mill, Aldine vicinity, N.J., early 18th century.

South elevation, carriage shed, Squire William Sever House, Kingston, Mass., early 19th century. Note the use of a fancy transom over the main entrance. All doors, however, are of simple sheathed construction.

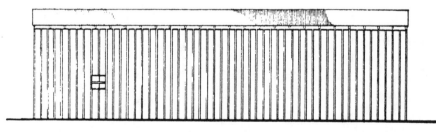

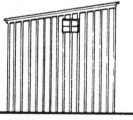

South elevation.

West elevation, carriage, saddle and harness house, "U Lazy S" Ranch, Post vicinity, Tex., late 19th century. The two-story box and strip building provides room for surreys and buggies in the center, tack rooms for saddles and harnesses at one end, and a feed-storage room at the other end. The second floor was used for general storage.

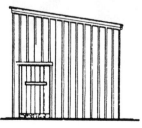

North elevation.

Wagon shed and corn crib, Walter-Kautz farm, Shawnee on Delaware vicinity, Pa., mid-19th century. The upper portion of this bank structure constitutes the wagon shed; the lower contains a built-in corn crib. The rolling doors to the shed are typical features.

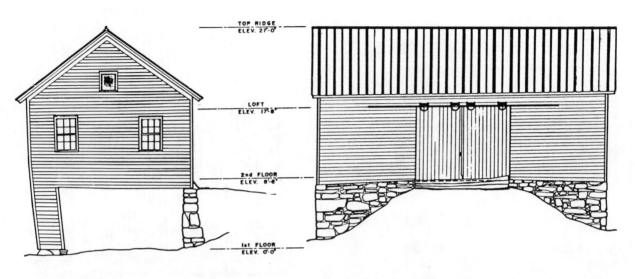

West elevation.

South elevation.

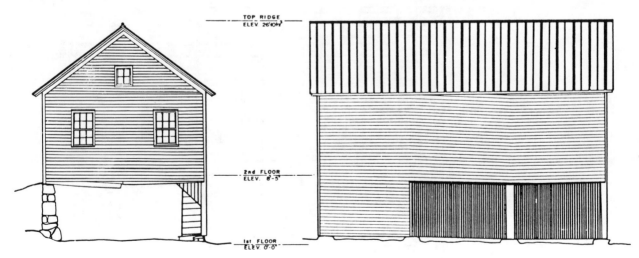

East elevation.

North elevation.

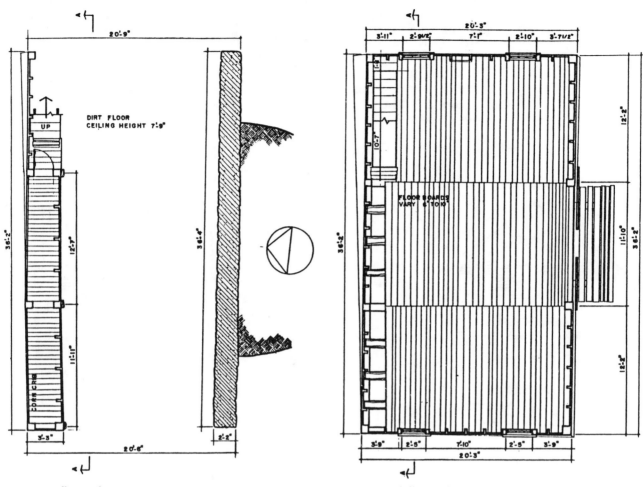

DIRT FLOOR
CEILING HEIGHT 7'-9"

First-floor plan.

FLOOR BOARDS
VARY 6" TO 10"

Second-floor plan.

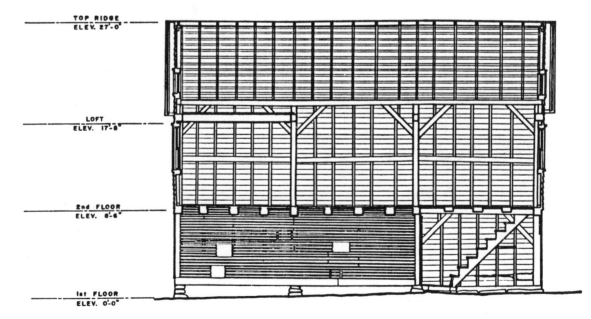

TOP RIDGE
ELEV. 27'-0"

LOFT
ELEV. 17'-8"

2nd FLOOR
ELEV. 8'-6"

1st FLOOR
ELEV. 0'-0"

Sectional view.

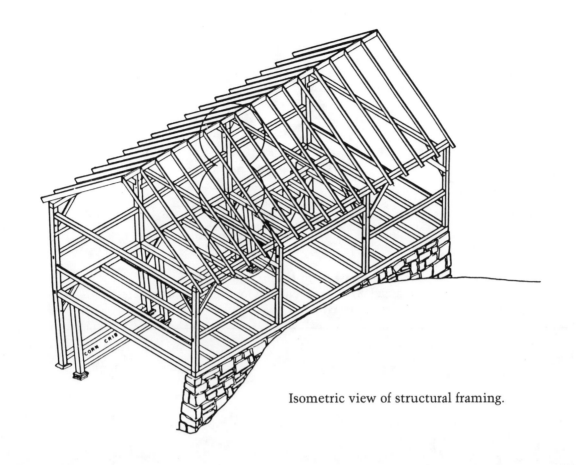

Isometric view of structural framing.

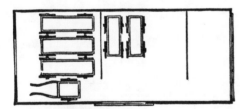

First-floor plan.

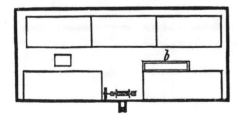

Second-floor plan.

Carriage, wagon, and tool house from *Barn Plans and Outbuildings* (Orange Judd Co., 1882). The second floor is to serve as a granary.

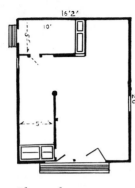

Floor plan.

Carriage house from *Home Building* by E. C. Hussey (1876), large enough for one or two vehicles, a horse, and a cow.

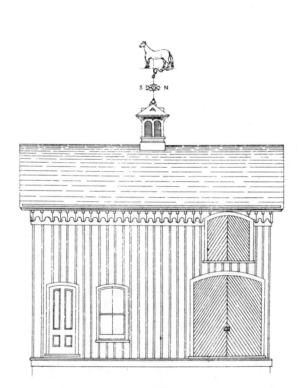

Side elevation, carriage house from *Supplement to Bicknell's Village Builder* by A. J. Bicknell (1871), with provision for two horses, a carriage, and second-floor storage.

Front elevation.

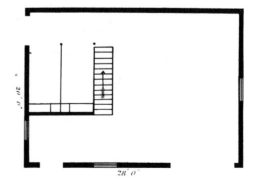

First-floor plan.

Rendering, carriage house from *Palliser's New Cottage Homes and Details* (Palliser, Palliser & Co., 1887), suitable for a suburban or country property.

Front elevation.

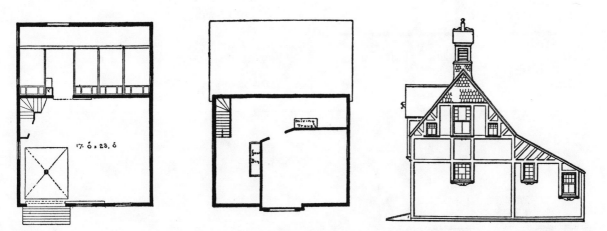

First-floor plan.

Second-floor plan.

Side elevation.

Carriage house from *Home Building* by E. C. Hussey (1876), fit for two horses and two or three vehicles.

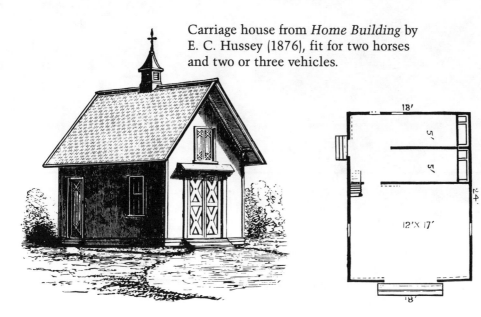

First-floor plan.

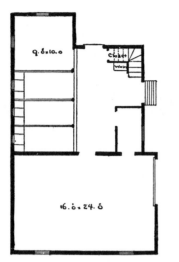

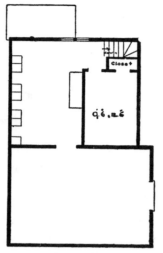

Carriage house from *Palliser's New Cottage Homes and Details* (Palliser, Palliser & Co., 1887), with ample room for three or more horses, two carriages, and a groom's room as well as storage space above.

First-floor plan.

Second-floor plan.

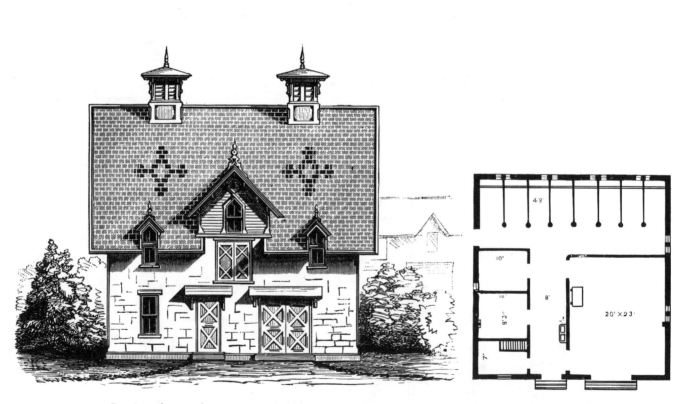

Carriage house from *Home Building* by E. C. Hussey (1876). A very elegant three-story building of brownstone served as a stable and quarters for groomsmen. The green slate roof contains blue-black accents; the doors are of oak.

Floor plan.

Front elevation, open shed and wagon shed,
Johnsonburg, N.J., early 19th century. The sheds are
attached to a stone barn and all three units are
built into the side of a hill. The tin roof was
originally wood shingled.

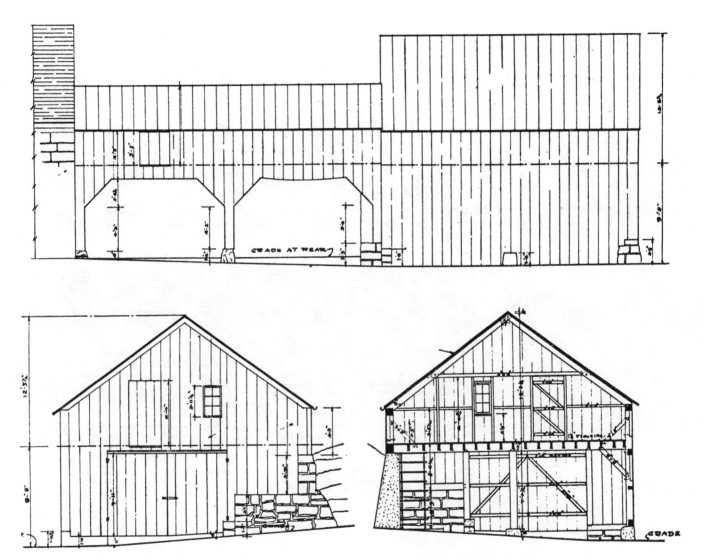

Rear elevation, wagon shed.

Cross-section, wagon shed.

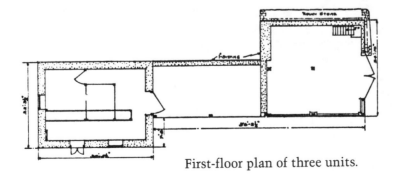

First-floor plan of three units.

19

First-floor plan of sheds. Both units have earth floors.

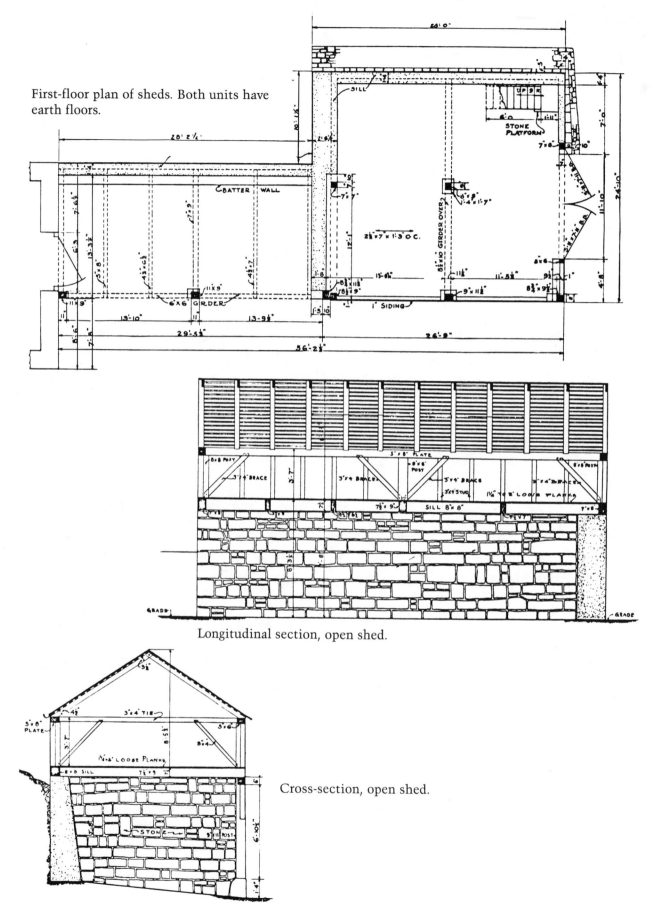

Longitudinal section, open shed.

Cross-section, open shed.

2. Doghouses

Special homes for man's best friend rarely receive much attention. A plain wooden crate usually has been the solution, no matter what the architecture of the period. A working country dog who spends most of his time in the outdoors, however, is deserving of extra care. "The dog is frequently left to find shelter as best he can," lamented one thoughtful Victorian, "on the lee side of the house or barn, or under the barn." Yet, the dog is sagacious enough "to know when he is well or ill treated, and he may very reasonably lose his self-respect, and take to evil courses . . . when not taught better, and provided with decent quarters at home." Four attractive and practical solutions to the canine dilemma are shown below. On the following page are drawings of the elegant apartment provided for one privileged Adams family pet at its owners' Quincy, Massachusetts, homestead.

Kennel designs from *Barn Plans and Outbuildings* (Orange Judd Co., 1881). Clockwise from upper right: a house measuring 4' long by 2'6" wide, 3'4" high in front, and 8" lower in the rear; a house 4' long, 2'6" wide, and 3'9" high, fitted with an arched-topped door ranging in size (depending on the occupant) from 8" wide by 12" high to 12" wide by 22" high; a yard and kennel for several canines with a pool at the left for bathing; a kennel measuring 7' long by 3'6" wide, with two doors, one opening inward and the other outward, and a bell to sound an exit.

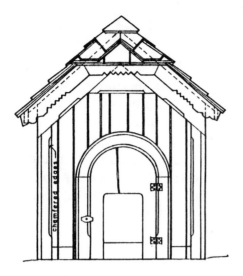

South elevation, doghouse, Adams National Historic Site, Quincy, Mass., early 19th century. A clipped gabled roof of wood shingles distinguishes this aristocratic kennel of the presidential Adams family. The First Dog deserved no less. The clapboard siding is a gray color and the trim is brown. The structure measures 2'10'' wide, 4'1¼'' long, and 3'5⅛'' high.

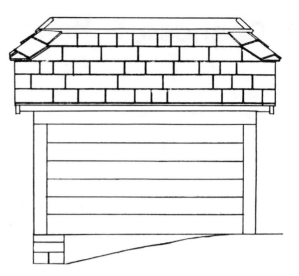

West elevation.

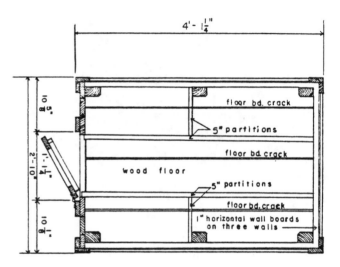

Floor plan.

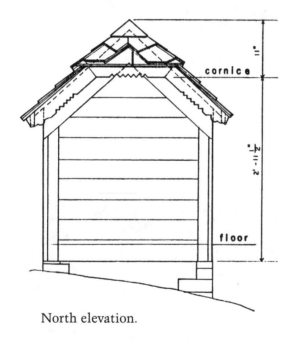

North elevation.

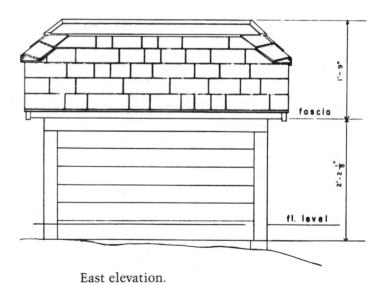

East elevation.

3. Gazebos, Summerhouses, and Greenhouses

A summerhouse provides an attractive vantage point from which to enjoy the garden or a picturesque landscape. Provided with seats and open to refreshing breezes, this type of small structure first became popular in the 18th century. During the Victorian era, the term *gazebo* was substituted for *summerhouse*, and this name continues in use today. The summerhouse or gazebo is usually fanciful in form, a majority being octagonal structures with a steeped pitched roof topped by a finial. Larger versions of this basic design were built as bandstands in public parks during the late 1800s and early 1900s. A greenhouse was rarely found in colonial America except on a few Southern estates. Only in the late Victorian era did a conservatory for plants, usually a part of the main house rather than a separate building, become at all common.

Summerhouse, The Vale, Waltham, Mass., early 1800s. The octagonal building has a fieldstone foundation and is painted yellow. The two-tiered roof is covered with cut wood shingles.

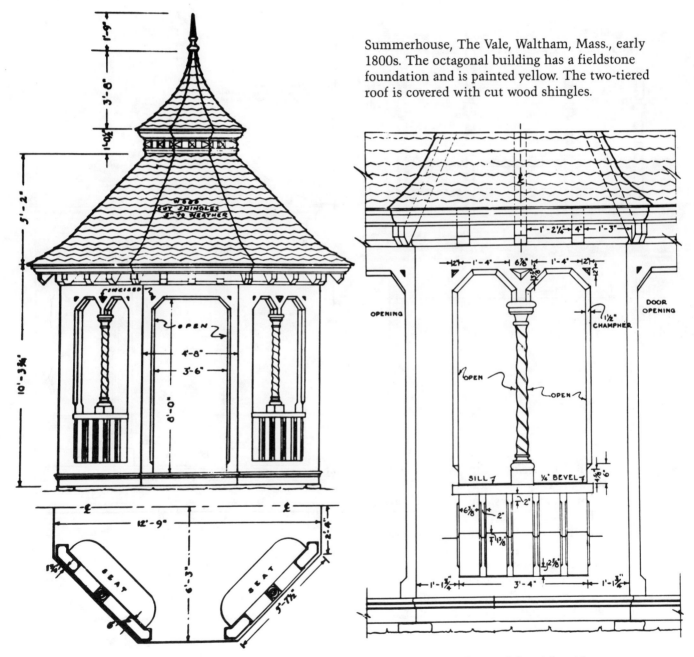

Floor plan with two of the four wood seats delineated.　　Sectional view of one of the eight sides.

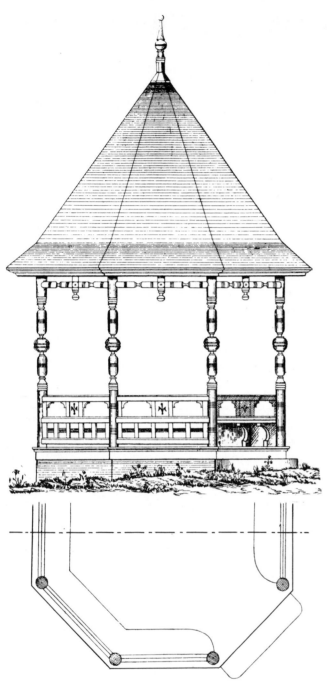

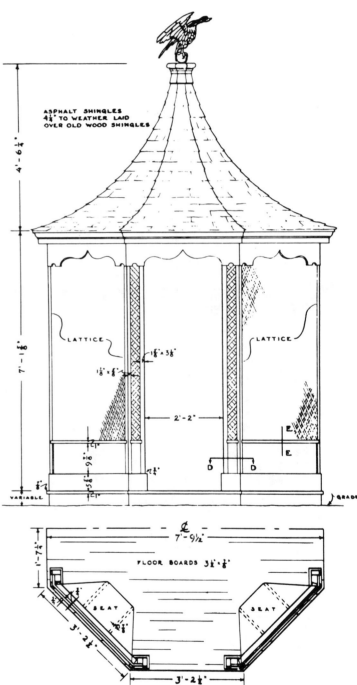

Summerhouse, John Cabot Place, Beverly, Mass., 1781. Latticework is used to screen six panels of the octagonal structure. Like the summerhouse shown on the opposite page, the building is completely open on two sides and is equipped with four seats. All the wood parts are painted gray; the roof is covered with wood shingles.

Gazebo, from *Modern Architectural Designs and Details*, by William T. Comstock and A. J. Bicknell (1881). The form remains the same in this design as it was earlier in the century, although elaborately turned columns, incised decoration, and pendants give the design a decided Queen Anne or Eastlake appearance. The gazebo rests on a brick foundation which is enclosed with wood panels. The roof is of wood shingles. Seating, as shown in the floor plan above, consists of a continuous wooden bench supported by brackets around seven sides of the building.

Summerhouse design from *The Art of Beautifying Suburban Home Grounds* by Frank J. Scott (1870). Hexagonal designs for such garden buildings were as popular as octagonal ones. The double roof and fretwork spandrels lend the building a romantic feeling befitting its use.

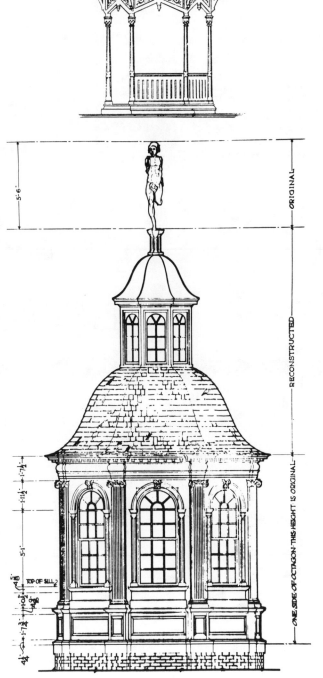

Summerhouse, Ashhurst estate, Mount Holly, N.J., early 19th century. The Chinese fretwork panels, used in place of the usual latticework, and the pagoda form suggest that this building was designed to be used as a teahouse.

Garden house, Col. Isaac Royal property, Medford, Mass., mid-18th century. The design of this very early building derives from European models.

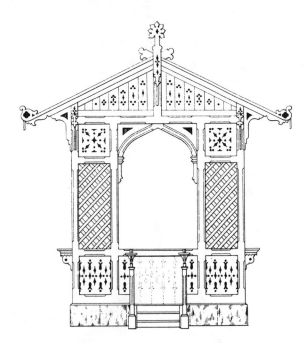

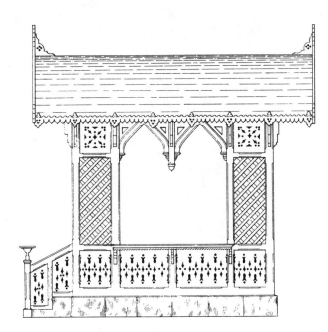

Front elevation, Swiss summerhouse design from *Detail, Cottage, and Constructive Architecture* (A. J. Bicknell & Co., 1873). Designs of this type had been popular in America since A. J. Downing introduced them in the 1840s.

Side elevation.

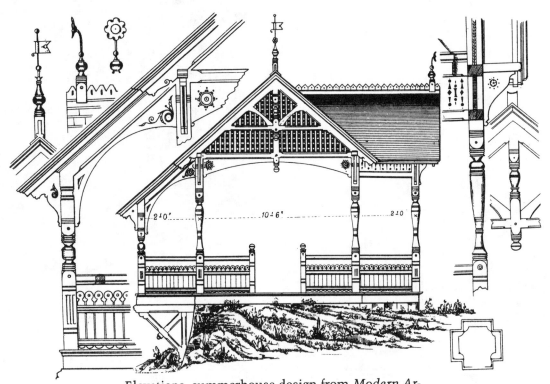

Elevations, summerhouse design from *Modern Architectural Designs and Details* by William T. Comstock and A. J. Bicknell (1881). The Queen Anne model was designed to be imaginatively positioned on a rocky promontory.

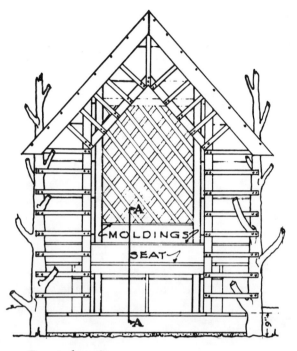

Front elevation.

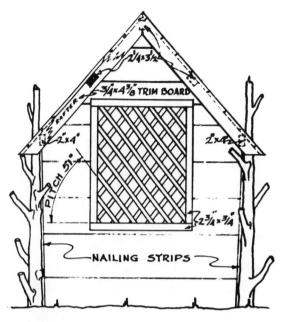

Rear elevation.

Rustic shelter, Gov. Jonathan Belcher Place, Milton,
Mass., early to mid-19th century. Red cedar posts
are set at the four corners and project through the
roof boards.

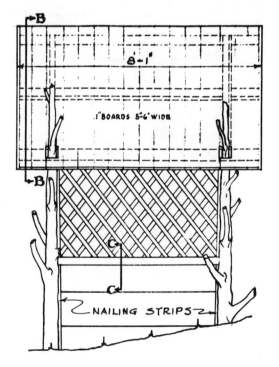

Side elevation.

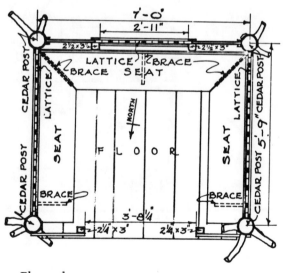

Floor plan.

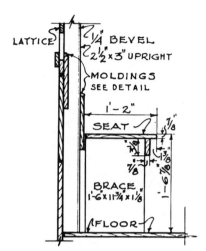

Sectional view of seat.

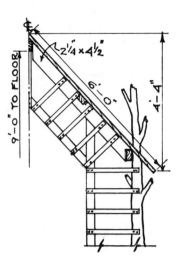

Sectional view of corner post and splats.

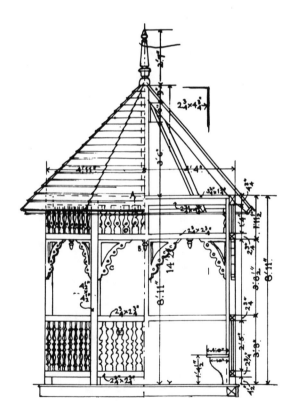

Half-elevation and half-sectional view, summerhouse, "Boulder Farm," Hopkinton, N.H., mid-19th century. Fancy spindles, drops, and spandrels embellish this six-sided retreat. Seats are positioned on five sides.

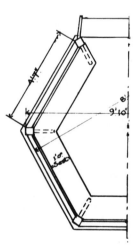

Half-floor plan.

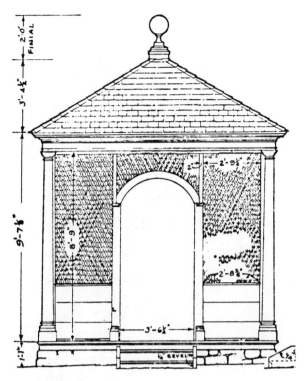

Front elevation.

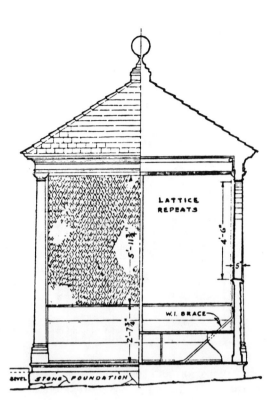

Rear elevation and sectional view.

Summerhouse, Gov. Jonathan Belcher Place,
Milton, Mass., 1780s. The building was painted red
to match the main house. Shutters were once used
on each side of the door and at the window at the
rear; these were painted green.

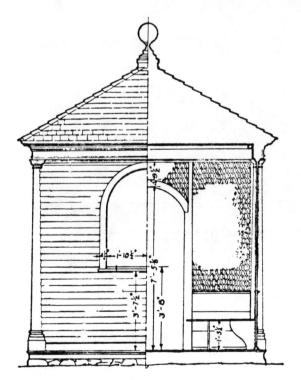

Side elevation and sectional view.

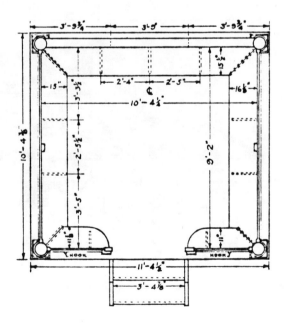

Floor plan.

29

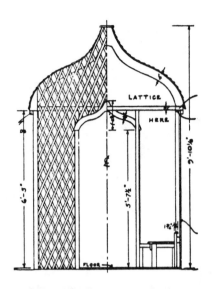

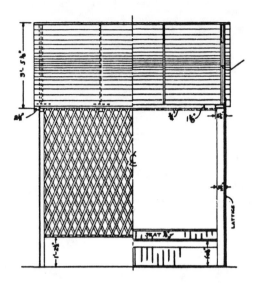

Side elevation and sectional view.

Front elevation and sectional view, summerhouse, Hodges-Peele-West residence, Salem, Mass., c. 1848. Persian in inspiration, the design of this airy garden structure is based on the ogee arch. The summerhouse was originally painted dark green and the shiplap roof boards were stained brown.

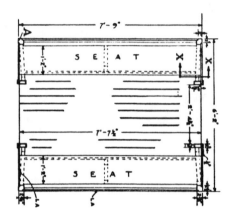

Floor plan.

Elevation, greenhouse, Wye House, Talbot County, Md., late 18th century. One of the earliest known greenhouses in America, this brick building is stuccoed and rusticated to resemble stone. It faces south to take full advantage of sunlight and at one time had a sophisticated hot-air system heated by a wood-burning furnace.

4. Icehouses

An icehouse was once as indispensable for a well-run farm as a barn or wagon shed. It was, essentially, a gigantic refrigerator used not only for storing blocks of ice but, often, for preserving dairy and meat supplies as well. During the coldest winter months, the building was stocked anew from nearby ice ponds; the supply of ice usually lasted until winter arrived again. Although frame icehouses were not unknown, the majority seem to have been built at least partially of stone or brick. Exterior walls were of double thickness and filled with such materials as sawdust or tanbark. The buildings were usually sited in a north-south direction, and were frequently half-buried in a hillside. The only opening in the walls was a door or two; ventilation was provided through the roof or holes positioned just under the eaves.

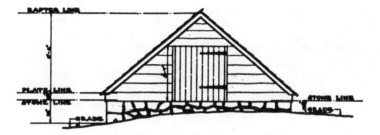

Front elevation, icehouse, Wright farm, Wrightsville, N.J., early 19th century. Half buried in a hillside, the building is barely visible from the front. The only openings are at the front and rear.

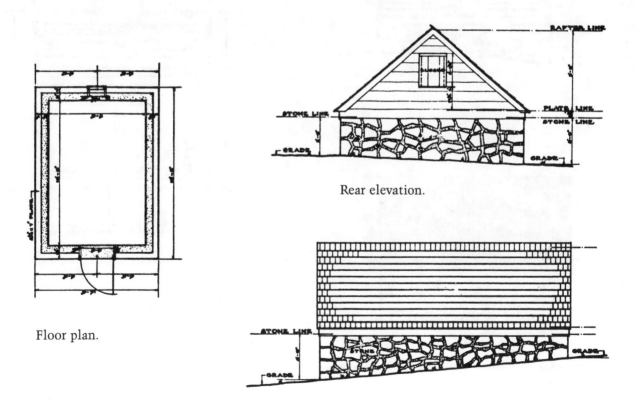

Rear elevation.

Floor plan.

Side elevation.

Front elevation, icehouse, Walter-Kautz farm, Shawnee on Delaware vicinity, Pa., early 19th century. The upper level was probably used for ice storage and the lower as a cooling room. Like other icehouses, this building burrows into the ground.

Sectional view.

Rear elevation.

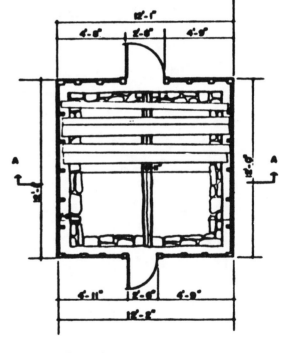

Floor plan.

Side elevation.

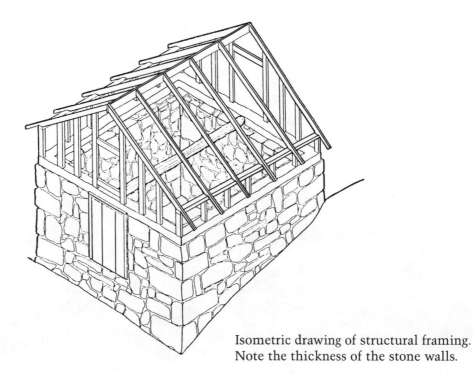

Isometric drawing of structural framing.
Note the thickness of the stone walls.

Elevation, icehouse, Wick farm, Delaware Township, N.J., early 19th century. An octagonal icehouse is an architectural novelty. This building predates the fashion for eight-sided structures which Orson Squire Fowler popularized in the 1840s and '50s. The underground level is circular in form.

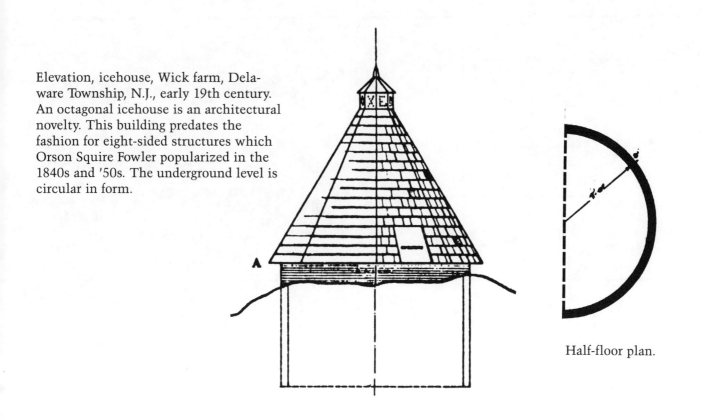

Half-floor plan.

Rendering, icehouse from *Barn Plans and Outbuildings* (Orange Judd Co., 1881). Storage space for ice was provided on the top floor, a level easily reached by delivery wagon. The roof has extra wide eaves to shade the walls. Below is a cooling room.

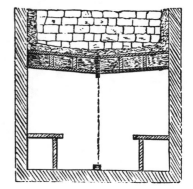

Rendering, cooling room, with shelves along the sides and a drainage pipe for waste water in the center.

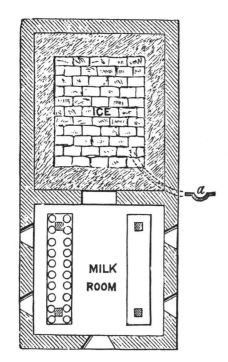

Floor plan.

Rendering, icehouse from *Barn Plans and Outbuildings*. The rear portion, nestled in the hillside, was to be used for storing ice; the front room was a dairy.

5. Offices

A farm office was a luxury only the most prosperous landowner could afford. The business affairs attendant to managing the average operation could be conducted easily at the kitchen table and were often performed by the farmer's wife. Overseers of vast ranches or extensive plantations, however, sometimes worked at an office separate from the house for a good part of each day. Such offices, nevertheless, were relatively modest in scale, usually being only one room wide and deep. The interior appointments were few, a fireplace being provided in the earliest buildings and a stove in the later ones. Other offices in country villages of the Colonial period, used by doctors and other professionals, were also small and modestly appointed (such as the Tayloe property shown below).

South elevation.

East elevation.

Tayloe Office, Williamsburg, Va., 18th century.

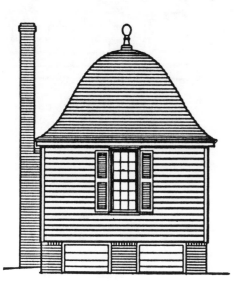

North elevation.

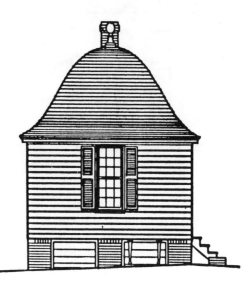

West elevation.

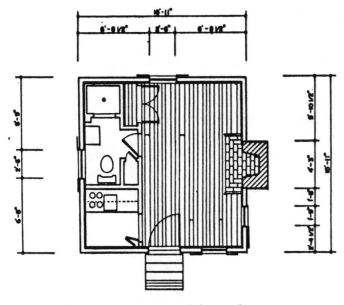

Floor plan, as arranged for modern use.

Detail of finial.

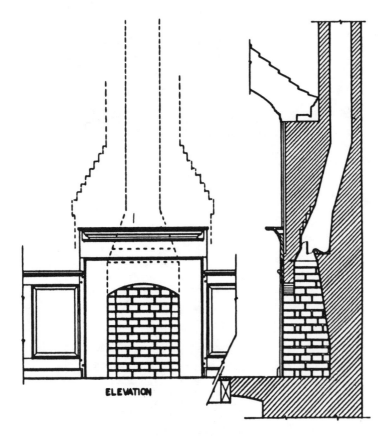

ELEVATION

Details of fireplace and flue.

Details of fireplace and hearth.

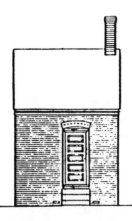

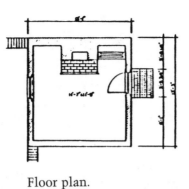

Floor plan.

South elevation.

Front elevation, office, Westover plantation, Charles City vicinity, Va., mid-18th century. Like other buildings of its type, the Westover office is only one room. This was sufficient space for completing paperwork, storing farm records, and meeting with buyers and vendors.

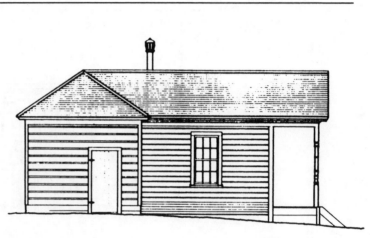

Side elevation.

Front elevation, Laguna Seca Rancho office, Coyote vicinity, Calif., late 19th century. The extensive ranch was a prosperous grain and livestock operation, one requiring careful management. The three-room office was a necessary central headquarters for owner Fiacro Fisher and his managers.

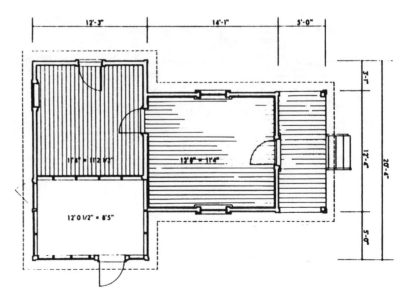

Floor plan.

Front elevation, farm office building, Wright farm, Wrightsville, N.J., 1832. A high-style Georgian Colonial building with unusual cast-iron decoration, this farm office was fit for a wealthy proprietor. The attic and basement levels were used for storage. Supplies could be hoisted up at one gable end. The main walls are of sandstone, a stucco finish remaining in some areas. Farm operations were overseen from the one-room main level.

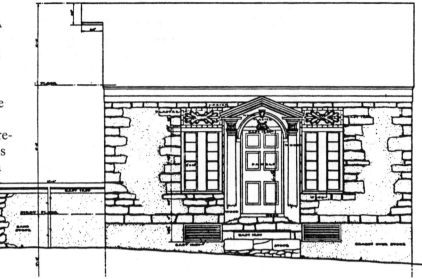

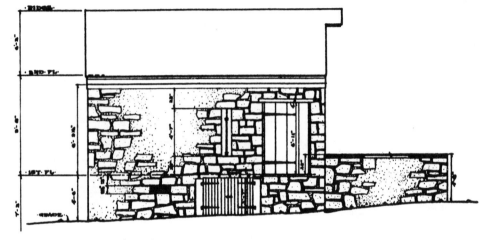

Rear elevation.

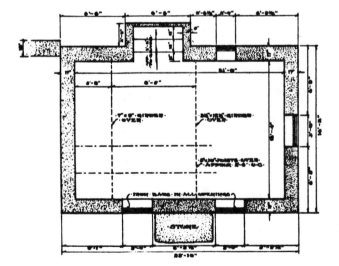

Basement floor plan.

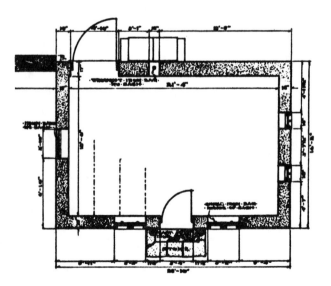

First-floor plan.

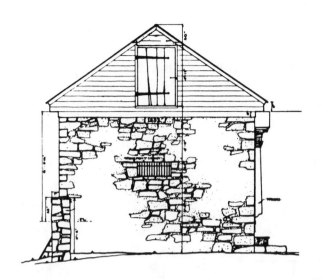

Side elevation.

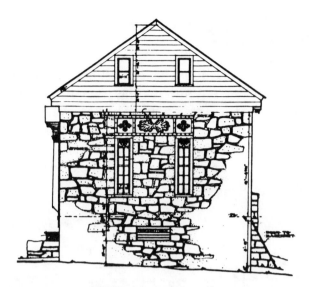

Side elevation.

Elevation of doorway.

6. Privies

The privy or outhouse has sometimes been called—with good reason—the necessary. Whether in town or country, no outbuilding was more important before the advent of modern plumbing. But there are privies and there are privies. The Byrds of Westover in the Virginia Tidewater built a very elaborate and comfortable necessary (see p. 43); so, too, did Judge Holten of Danvers, Massachusetts (see facing page). The privy illustrated below was the type found in most American backyards or farmyards—a simple two-seater. The privy was usually located close to the main house for obvious convenience, especially on cold winter nights.

Front elevation, Ambrose Snow privy, Truro, Mass., 19th century. Appropriately shingled, this Cape Cod two-seater is a sturdy, strictly functional structure.

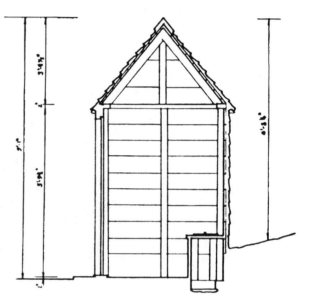

Sectional view.

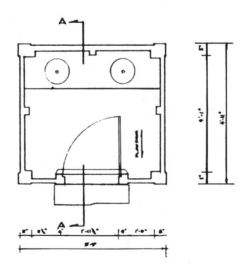

Floor plan.

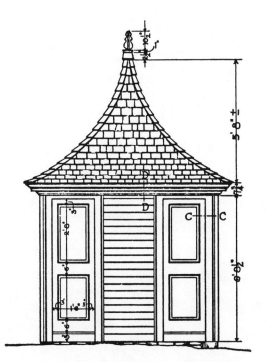

Front elevation, Judge Samuel Holten privy, Danvers, Mass., early 19th century. Known as a back-to-back model, this privy is handsomely ornamented and comfortably equipped for adults and

Side elevation.

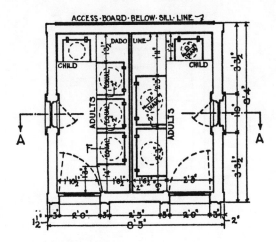

Floor plan.

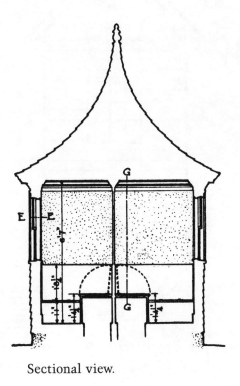

Sectional view.

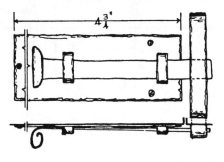

Detail of thumb latch used for doors.

children. The interior walls are finished—from top to bottom—with a wood cornice, plaster, and wood wainscoting.

41

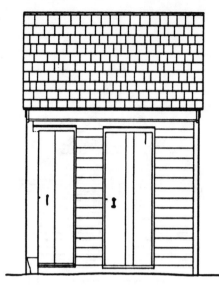

Front elevation, Archibald Blair privy,
Williamsburg, Va., 19th century.

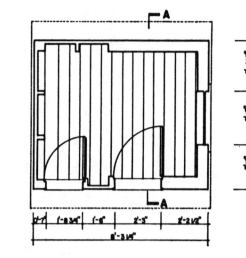

Floor plan.

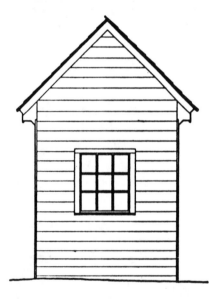

Side elevation.

Sectional view.

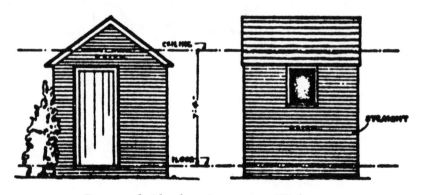

Front and side elevations, privy, Wick
farm, Delaware Township, N.J., early 19th
century.

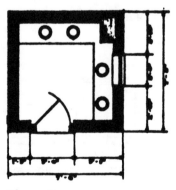

Floor plan.

42

Front and side elevations, privy, Westover, Charles City vicinity, Va., mid-18th century. From the ex-

terior, the privy looks very much like the other out-buildings on the plantation. It is, however, quite luxurious, boasting a fireplace in addition to the five seats, three of which are arranged in a semicircle.

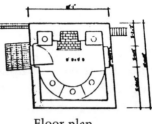

Floor plan.

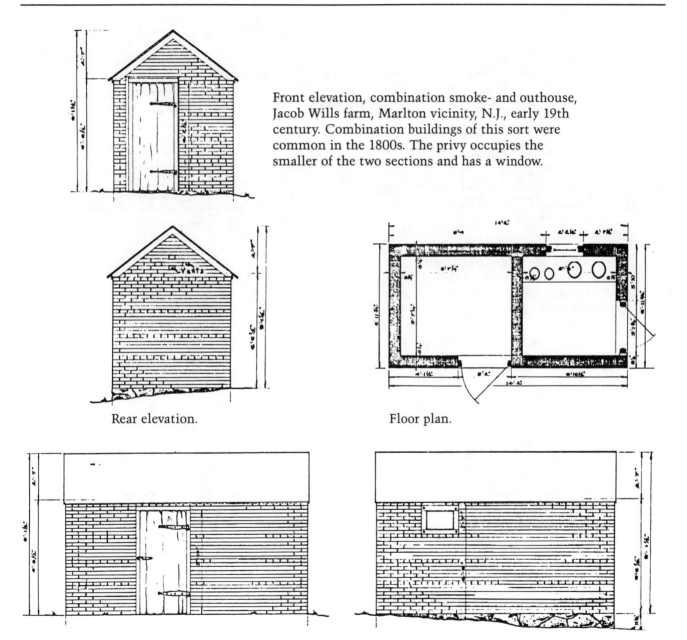

Rear elevation.

Front elevation, combination smoke- and outhouse, Jacob Wills farm, Marlton vicinity, N.J., early 19th century. Combination buildings of this sort were common in the 1800s. The privy occupies the smaller of the two sections and has a window.

Floor plan.

Side elevation, showing smokehouse entrance.

Side elevation.

7. Smokehouses and Ovens

The curing of meat by smoking it was a common practice during the 18th and 19th centuries in America. This procedure for preserving perishables could be performed in something as small as a wooden barrel, but it was preferable to have a separate building in which to both cure and store the meat. A well-designed smokehouse was nearly airtight and usually had no windows, although allowance had to be made to vent the smoke properly. This was accomplished by using a flue or vents in the roof or under the eaves. The ideal building was constructed of brick or stone rather than inflammable wood. When wood was used, it was often limited to the upper portion of the building, where meat was hung to cure. The fire was always built at the lowest level, often below ground in a pit or special fireplace. Combination bake ovens and smokehouses were also constructed; the fire for one purpose could then provide the smoke for the other.

Front elevation, smokehouse, Clifford-Williamson homestead, Pattenburg vicinity, N.J., early 19th century. The solid stone, windowless rectangle is perfectly suited to serve the needs of a small farm family. Ventilation is provided through two small holes in the front and rear gables.

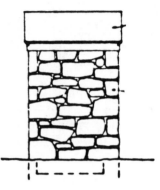

Side elevation.

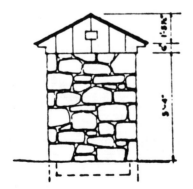

Rear elevation.

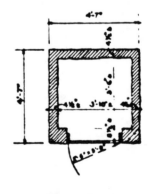

Floor plan.

44

Front elevation, smokehouse, Archibald Blair property, Williamsburg, Va., 18th century. Restored in 1930-31 by Colonial Williamsburg, this smokehouse presents a very neat appearance, a condition that probably did not prevail when it was in use. Round butt wood shingles have been used for the roof.

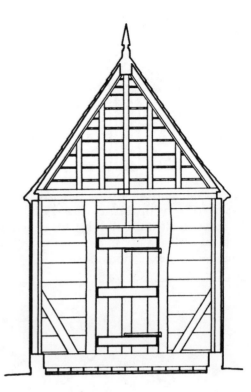

Sectional view.

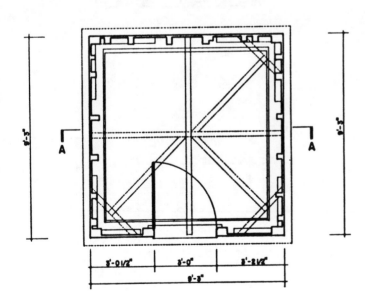

Floor plan.

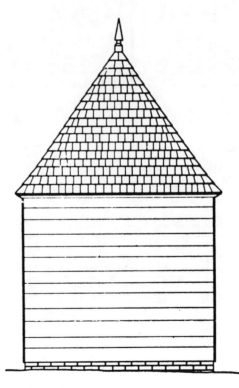

Side elevation.

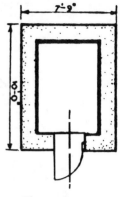

Front elevation, smokehouse, Squire Michael Porter farm, Sharon Township, Mich., early 19th century. A four-square fieldstone building, this smokehouse has a typical early American design; the arched entryway is the only exceptional feature.

Side elevation.

Floor plan.

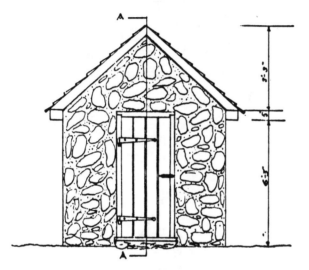

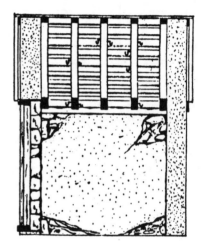

Front elevation, smokehouse, Richard Watson Gilder property, Bordentown, N.J., 18th century. As the other drawings indicate, this fieldstone building was once plastered over for insulation, as were many smokehouses.

Sectional view.

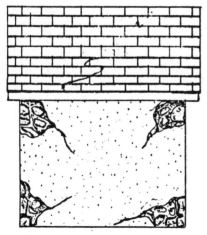

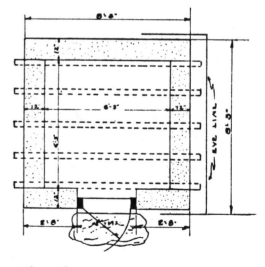

Side elevation.

Floor plan.

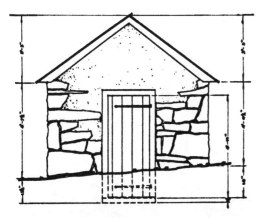

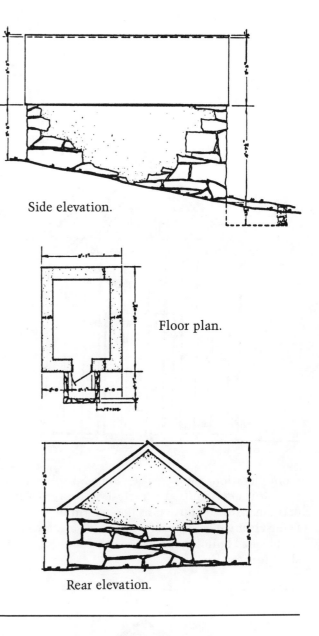

Side elevation.

Front elevation, smokehouse, William Meirs homestead, Cream Ridge, N.J. 18th century. This simple fieldstone smokehouse is sited in a hillside, thereby insulating it from changes in the outside temperature.

Floor plan.

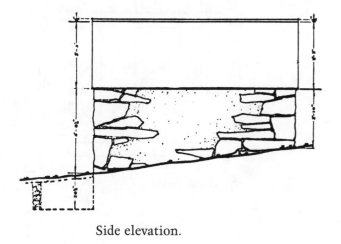

Side elevation.

Rear elevation.

Front elevation, smokehouse, Wick farm, Delaware Township, N.J., early 19th century. A chimney provided an outlet for the smoky fumes which were produced each time a fire was set.

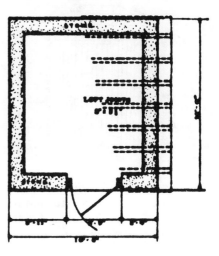

Floor plan

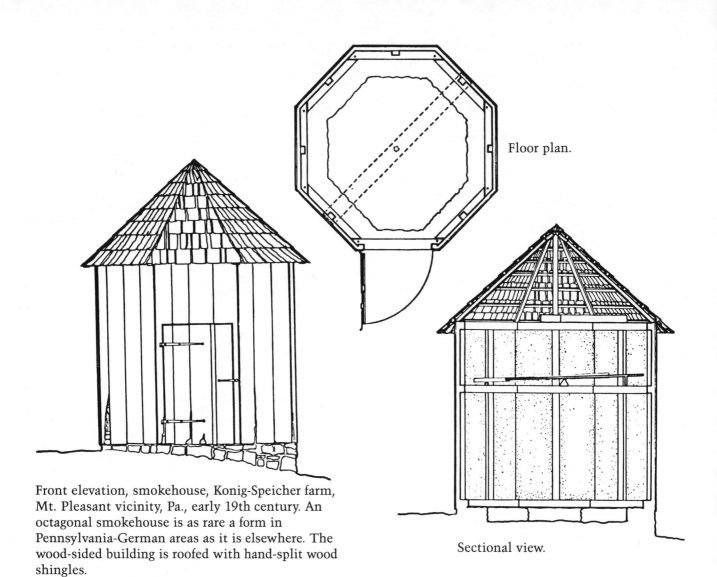

Floor plan.

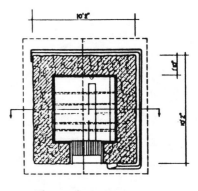

Sectional view.

Front elevation, smokehouse, Konig-Speicher farm, Mt. Pleasant vicinity, Pa., early 19th century. An octagonal smokehouse is as rare a form in Pennsylvania-German areas as it is elsewhere. The wood-sided building is roofed with hand-split wood shingles.

Floor plan.

Cross-section, smokehouse, John Turn farm, Shawnee on Delaware vicinity, Pa., early 19th century. A monolithic building, its two-foot-thick stone walls nestled in a slight incline, this smokehouse was still in use as late as the 1920s. Ventilation was provided in a gable-end opening.

Front elevation.

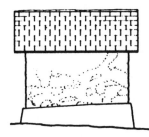

Side elevation.

Rear elevation.

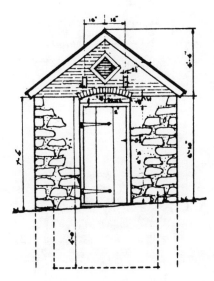

Front elevation.

Smokehouse, Wright farm, Wrightville, N.J., early 19th century. Like other buildings on the Wright property, the smokehouse was an ornamental as well as a functional structure. Diamond-shaped vents pierce each gable end; there is also a square opening on one side. The interior is vaulted.

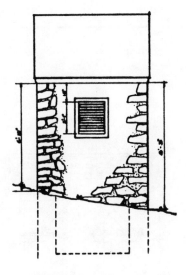

Side elevation.

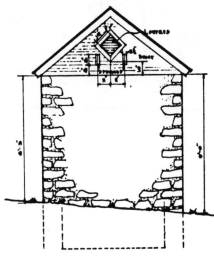

Rear elevation.

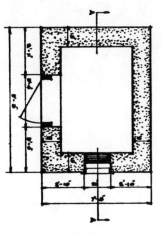

Floor plan.

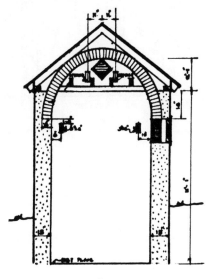

Sectional view.

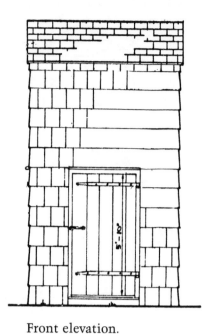

Front elevation.

Smokehouse, Corneles Couwenhoven House, Holmdel Township, N.J., 18th century. The elongated form of building is found on many early Dutch Colonial and Pennsylvania-German homesteads. The bottom area provided the fire chamber; the upper area, the smoke chamber.

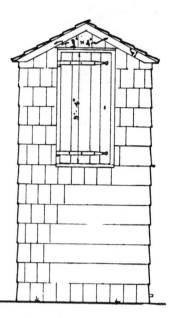

Rear elevation.

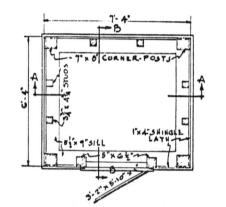

First-floor plan.

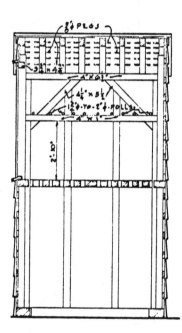

Sectional side view.

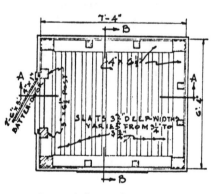

Second-floor plan.

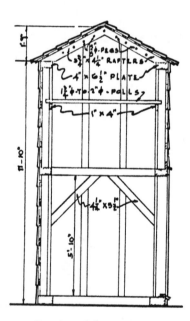

Sectional front view.

Front elevation, smokehouse, John Smith farm, Morris County, N.J., late 18th century. Special features of this fieldstone building are the off-center entrance, with a handsome board-and-batten door, and the vaulted interior. Meat was hung from built-in stringers along the width of the building.

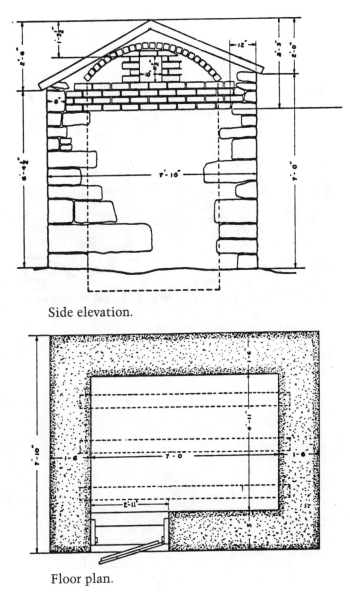

Side elevation.

Floor plan.

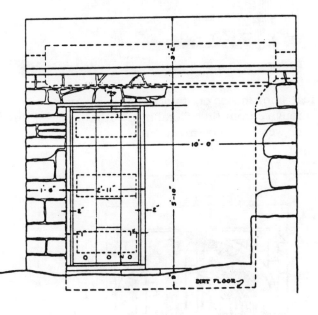

Front elevation, side elevation, and floor plan, smokehouse, Dundore farm, Mt. Pleasant vicinity, Pa., mid-19th century. This and many of the other outbuildings on a prosperous Pennsylvania-German farm were built of square logs and posts with diagonal braces.

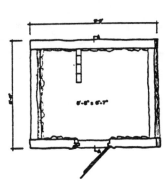

Front and rear views, combined oven and smokehouse from *Barn Plans and Outbuildings* (Orange Judd Co., 1881). The smoke produced by the fire set for baking could be channeled into the rear smokehouse or, if not needed, exhausted through a front flue. Combined outbuildings of this type were found on many farmsteads.

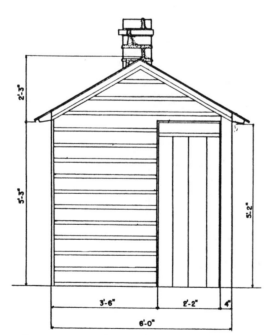 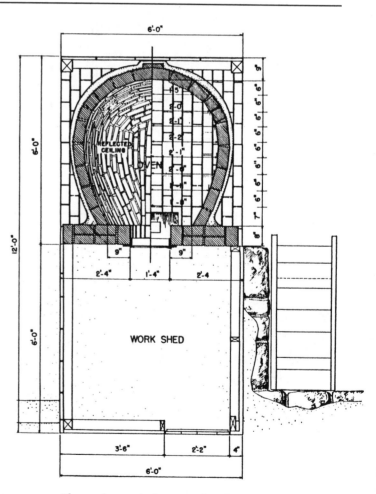

Front elevation, smokehouse and bake oven, Bricker farm, Gettysburg vicinity, Pa., early 19th century. Built on two levels, this combination oven and smokehouse makes practical use of the fire built at one end. The smokehouse section is built primarily of wood while the oven level makes use of brick and stone.

Floor plan at bake oven level.

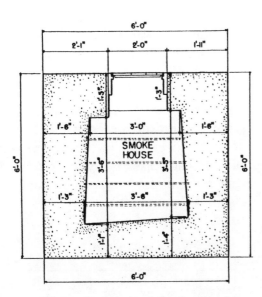

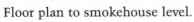

Floor plan to smokehouse level.

Sectional view.

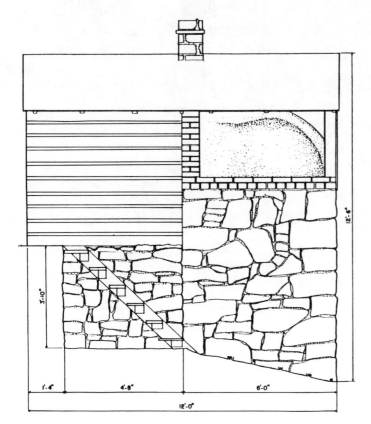

Side elevation.

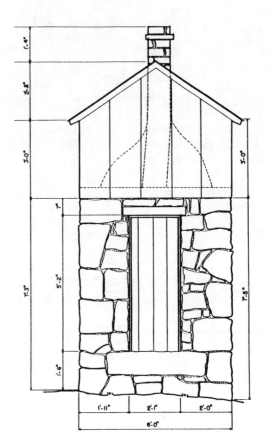

Rear elevation.

8. Springhouses and Dairies

Next to a privy and a shelter for animals, a springhouse was the most important outbuilding on many early farms. Building sites that were blessed with a free-flowing source of water were the first to be sold. At a time when automatic drilling equipment was still only a dream, the settlers thus had no immediate need of a hand-dug well; a natural spring was a valuable resource to be protected and used well. Some springhouses were built over the source; others were constructed nearby, with water fed into the building by the force of gravity. The troughs which lined the walls served as basins for keeping milk and other dairy products cool and fresh; the cool temperature also served well for the preservation of fruits and vegetables. The springhouse was also often used as a place to make cheese and butter, and thus served as a dairy. On farms where there was no natural spring, a building known as a dairy sometimes served the same purpose as the springhouse. In layout the buildings were similar. They were frequently constructed of stone, well lighted with one or more windows, and well ventilated.

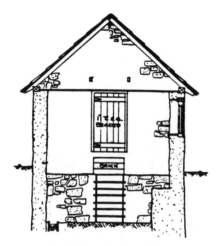

Front elevation, springhouse, Rockford, Lancaster vicinity, Pa., late 18th century. Well banked into a hillside, this springhouse is built primarily of stone. The walls are over two feet thick. A trough runs along two walls and is fed from a spring located in one corner.

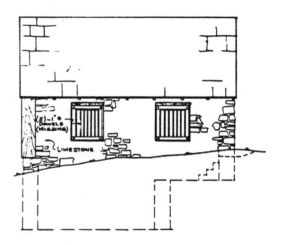

Side elevation.

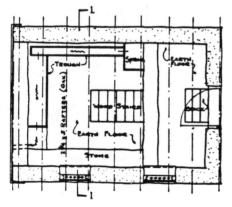

Floor plan.

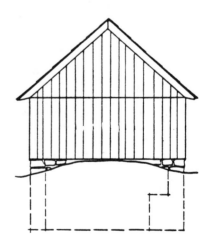

Rear elevation.

54

Dairy, Archibald Blair property, Williamsburg, Va., 18th century. Just how provisions were kept cool in this outbuilding is not clear, though the troughs to hold milk cans and pails which line each side were probably filled with cold water from a nearby well. Several aspects of the building's design contribute to keeping it cool—the wide roof overhang, brick floor, and louvered vents.

Front elevation.

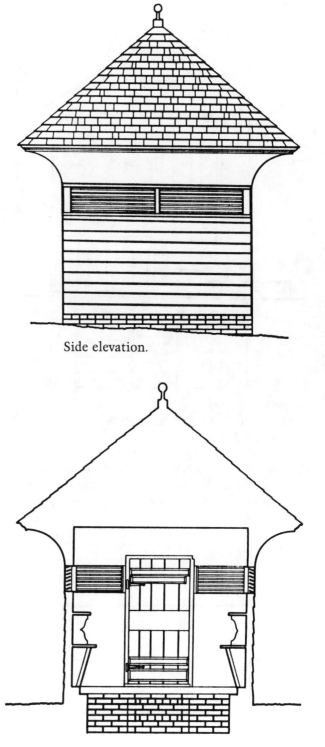

Side elevation.

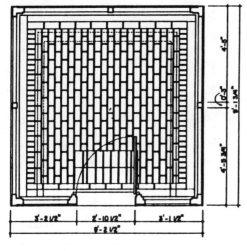

Floor plan.

Sectional view.

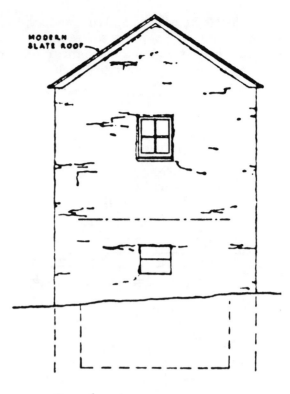

Rear elevation.

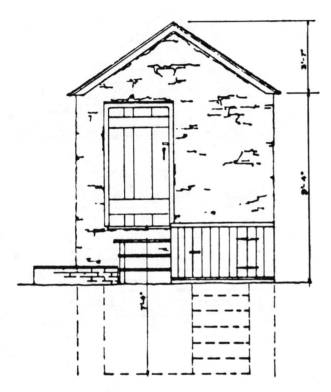

Front elevation, springhouse, Clifford-Williamson homestead, Pattenburg vicinity, N.J., early 19th century. The two-story building extends well into the ground. It is possible that the basement was used for storing dairy products; it is here that the spring was located. The main floor provided space for making cheese and butter.

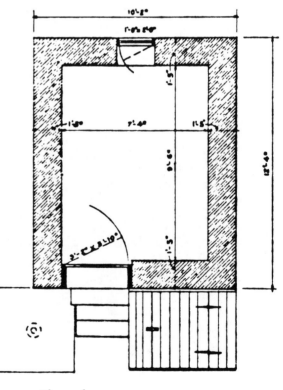

Floor plan.

Springhouse design from *Barn Plans and Outbuildings* (Orange Judd Co., 1881). According to Victorian experts of the time, a springhouse had to provide for "coolness of water, purity of air, preservation of an even temperature during all seasons, and perfect drainage." This building met all four criteria. There are two different suggested interior layouts. The arrangement with elevated troughs to carry the spring water is preferred, as it eliminates stooping over to deposit or remove heavy cans. If a spring was high enough, water could be piped in at this level. If, however, the spring was low, a trough nearly at ground level was the better solution. In either case, note that the walls are plastered and the floor is composed of stone paving blocks.

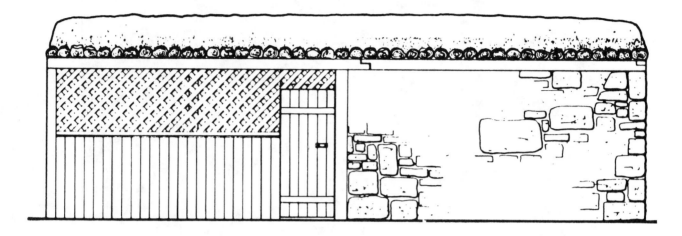

Front and rear elevations, milk and meat cooler,
J A Ranch, Claude vicinity, Tex., late 19th century.
Keeping perishables fresh in the dry plains area of
Texas was a particular problem. This building was
well designed for the purpose, with its plastered
stone walls, latticework, and mud-covered roof.
Milk and butter were stored in containers set in
cold running water, and meat was hung from the
rafters.

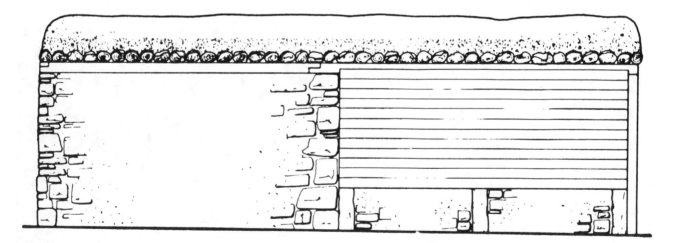

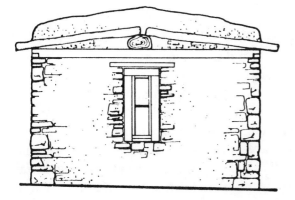

Side elevation.

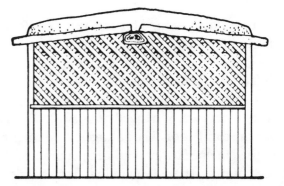

Side elevation.

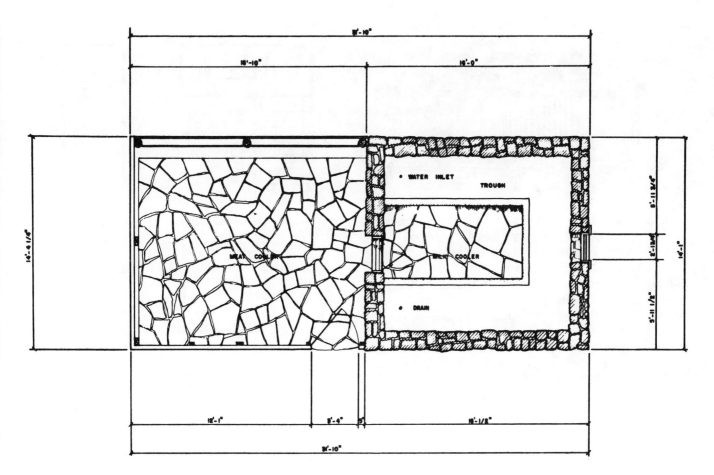

Floor plan.

9. Stables and Barns

The outbuildings found on any 18th- or 19th-century farm might be few or many, but every country property included a barn and/or stable. Stables were also found in villages and towns, and even small barns found a place on suburban lots. Both types of buildings were used for stabling horses and storing their feed, and included a loft for hay and straw storage. A barn, although in many cases not much larger than a horse stable, usually also provided space for at least one cow. Increasingly throughout the 19th century, barns were enlarged or newly built to include housing for such small animals as hens and pigs under the same roof. The enlarged barn might also serve as a place to thresh grain and as a granary. As explained in one farmer's building manual of the 1880s, "With the increase of wealth among the farmers of the country, there is a gradual but very decided improvement in farm architecture. . . . Compared with a well-arranged barn, a group of small buildings is inconvenient and extremely expensive to keep in good repair." Wonderful examples of barn architecture—large, well-built, multipurpose buildings— have survived the mechanization of the farm economy in the 20th century. Noteworthy among these buildings is a unique American type—the Pennsylvania bank or hillside barn—examples of which are illustrated in the following pages.

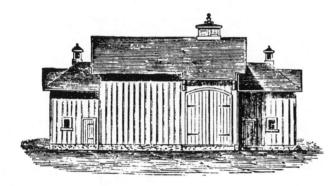

Grain and stock barn design from *Atwood's Country and Suburban Houses* by Daniel T. Atwood (1871). This attractive board-and-batten frame barn could serve as the headquarters for a large farm. Timber-framed, the building was designed with many different functions in mind. The central rectangle housed a threshing room and a granary on the first floor. The side wings, extending to an L shape behind the center section, provided for a wagon house, horse stalls, harness room, feed room, corn crib, pigpen, and hennery.

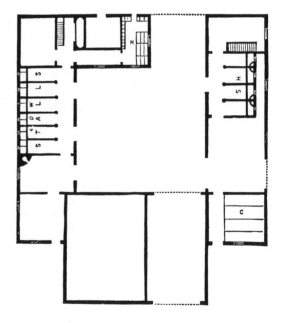

First-floor plan.

Barn, Squire Michael Porter farm, Sharon Township, Mich., early 19th century. The plastered limestone barn is unusual for its exceptional styling. The massive arched entryway is worthy of a church or university hall and provided ample space for the entry of teams of horses and livestock.

Front elevation.

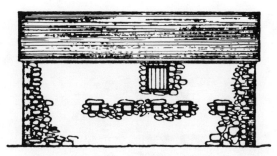

Side elevation.

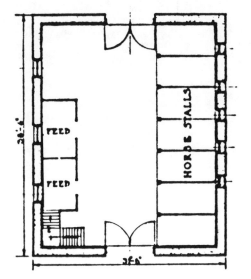

Floor plan.

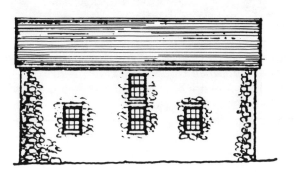

Side elevation.

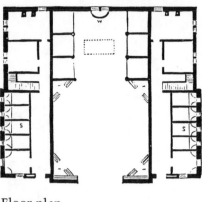

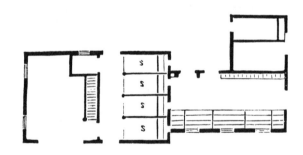

Floor plan.

Double stable design for D. D. Chamberlain farm, Croton Falls, N.Y., and published in *Atwood's Country and Suburban Houses* by Daniel T. Atwood (1871). Chamberlain was a country gentleman who possessed many horses and vehicles. There are stalls for ten horses and space enough in the center pavilion for at least four wagons and their maintenance. There is even a groom's room. The stable is built of brick.

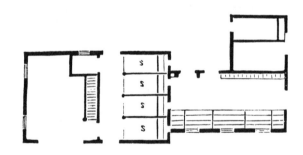

Floor plan.

Small suburban stable design from *Atwood's Country and Suburban Houses* by Daniel T. Atwood (1871). A more modest gentleman's stable is envisioned in this second Atwood plan; it is of a size better suited to a village setting. A carriage room, stalls, and harness closet are included in the main section to the left; at right is a henhouse and piggery.

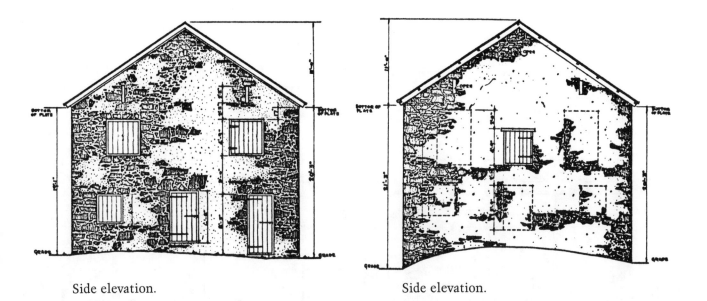

Side elevation.   Side elevation.

Barn, Tench Francis farm, Paulsboro vicinity, N.J.,
early 19th century. Like many early agricultural
buildings in the Delaware Valley, this large barn
was built of stone and plastered over. It is slightly
over 90′ wide, 31′ high, and 30′ deep. The ground
floor housed the horse stalls and feed-storage area,
and contained sufficient room for wagons. The second level was for hay storage. The vertical slits
supply ventilation for the hay mows.

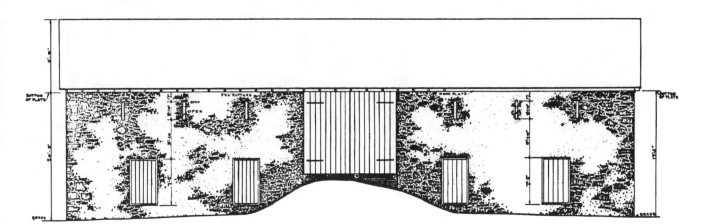

Front elevation.

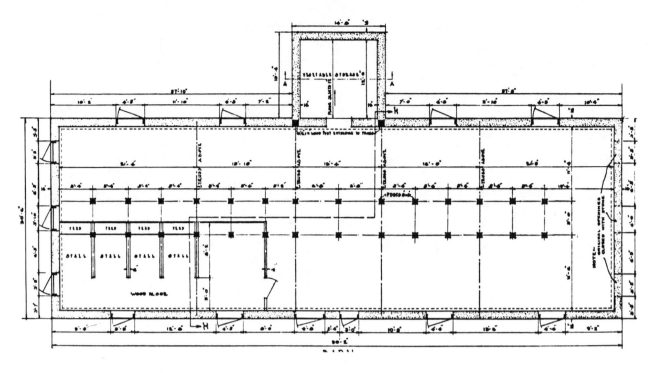

Ground-floor plan.

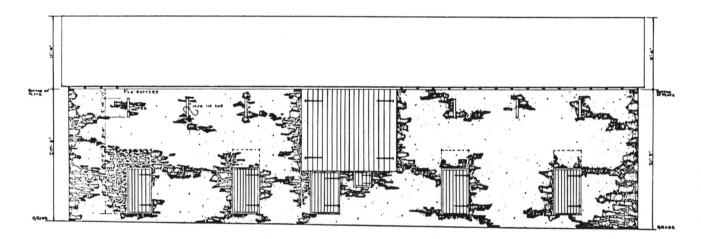

Rear elevation.

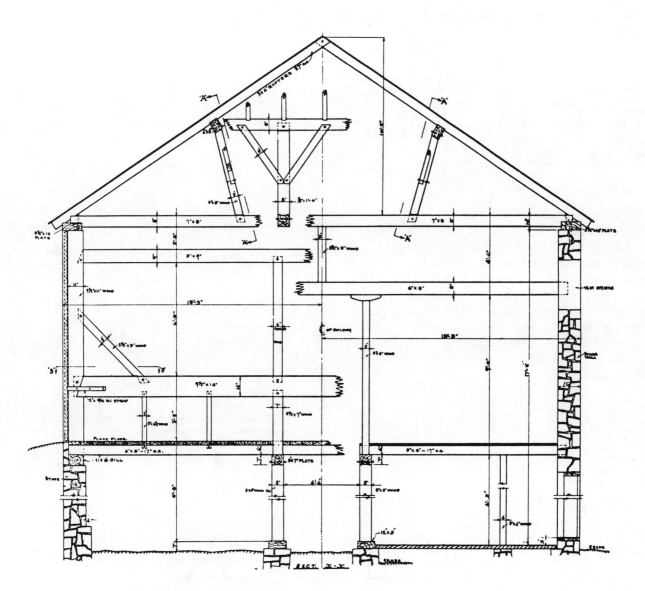

Sectional view; almost all the timber framing is
oak.

Front elevation, Ellis Stone barn, Wellesley, Mass., 18th century. Although termed a barn, there is little doubt that this building also served—if only for a short time—as a residence as well. In the early days of settlement, men and beasts often shared the same quarters. The walls of the two second-floor rooms are plastered. The building includes a chimney, but evidence of a fireplace has disappeared.

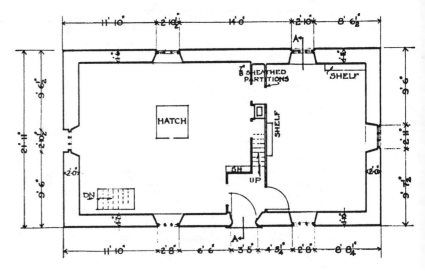

Second-floor plan.

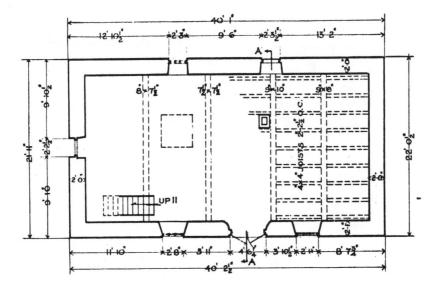

First-floor plan.

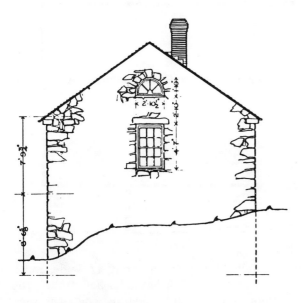

Side elevation.

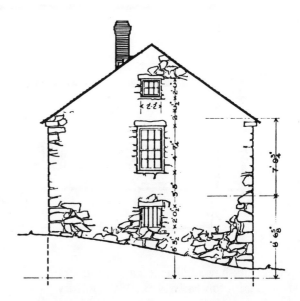

Side elevation; the first floor is nearly hidden in the hillside at the rear.

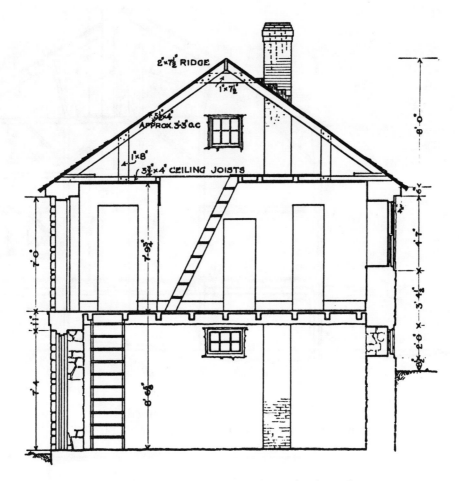

Sectional view; a primitive stairway leads to the loft, an area perhaps used for sleeping.

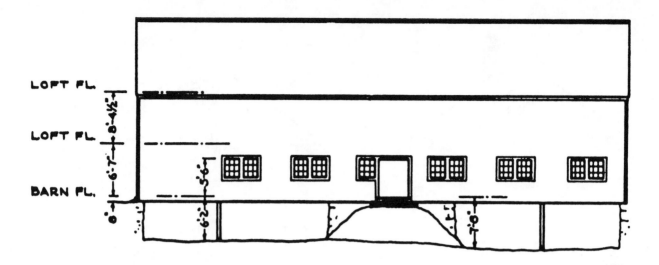

LOFT FL.

LOFT FL.

BARN FL.

Front elevation, hay and cattle barn, John Cram farmstead, Hampton Falls, N.H., 19th century. Shingles, 8″ to weather, cover the walls and roof of this New England barn. The bank structure is approximately 24′ high at the front, 17′ wide, and 100′ long. There are two loft levels for hay storage, the first-floor for cattle and threshing, and a basement which is partially usable.

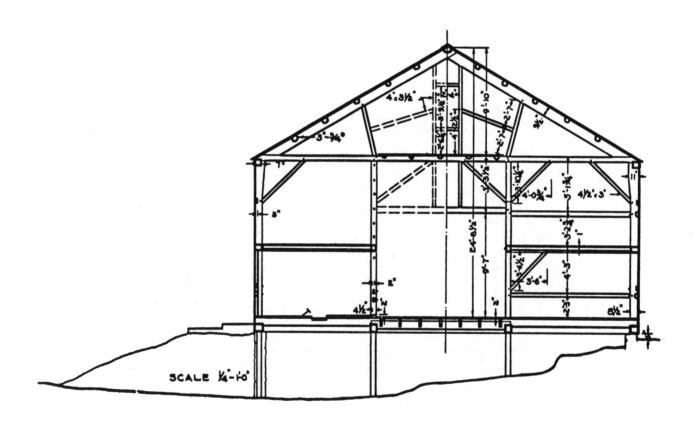

SCALE ¼″-1′0″

Sectional view; the barn is timber framed, and rungs on the posts are provided for climbing from one level to another.

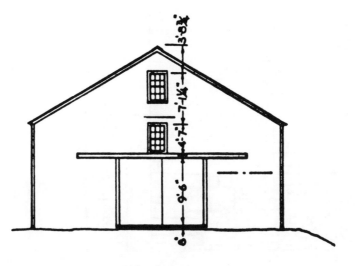

Side elevation.

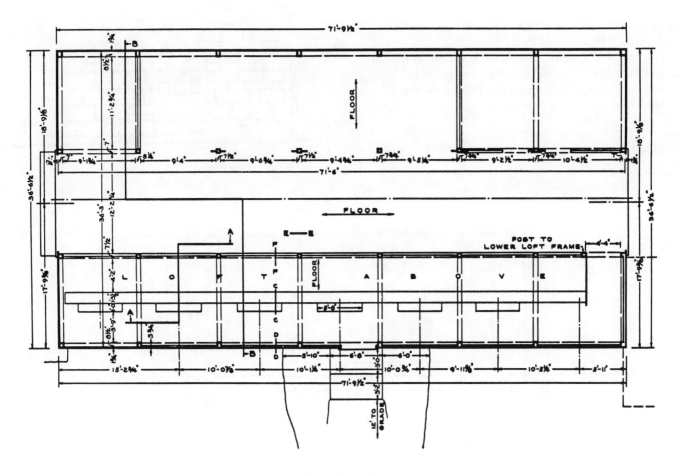

First-floor plan.

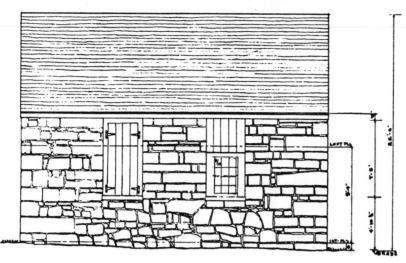

Side elevation.

Stone barn, Johnsonburg, N.J., 18th century. Approximately 21′ wide by 30′ long, this barn served the needs of a small farm. The first floor contains stalls for several cows or horses and room for feed, hay, and small equipment; the loft, reachable by ladder, was used for storing hay.

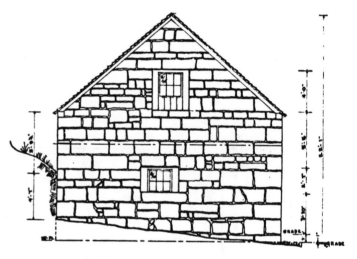

Rear elevation.

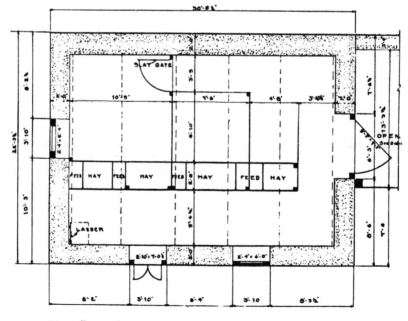

First-floor plan.

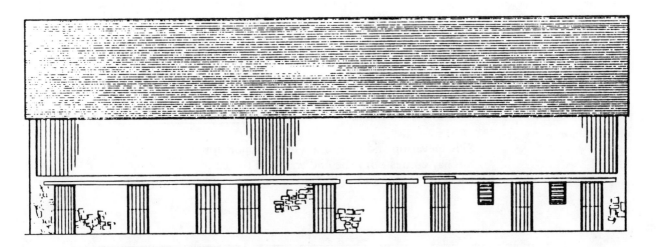

Rear elevation.

The Village Barn, Hopewell Village National
Historic Site, Berks County, Pa., reconstructed
1926. This Pennsylvania bank or, as it is sometimes
called, hillside barn, incorporates many typical
features of the type—a second-level frame overhang
known as a forebay, a ramp to the threshing floor
on the uphill side, and stables on the ground level.

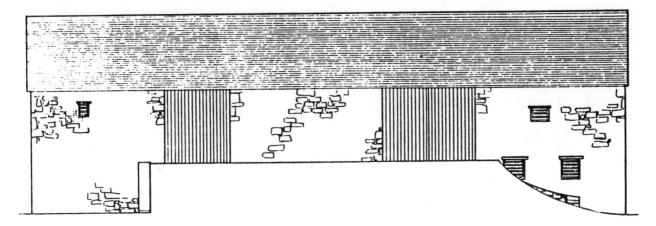

Front elevation.

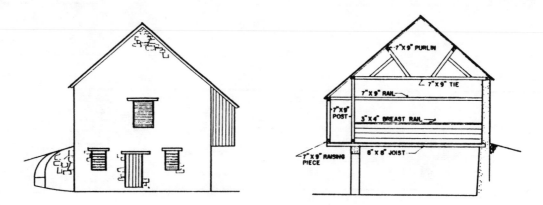

Side elevation and sectional view; support for the
forebay comes from the end wall and the can-
tilevered first-floor joists.

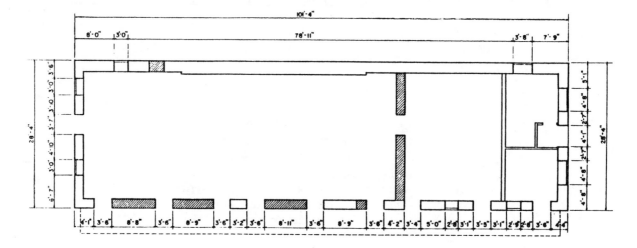

First-floor, stable plan; this level was divided into
stalls for cows, horses, and mules.

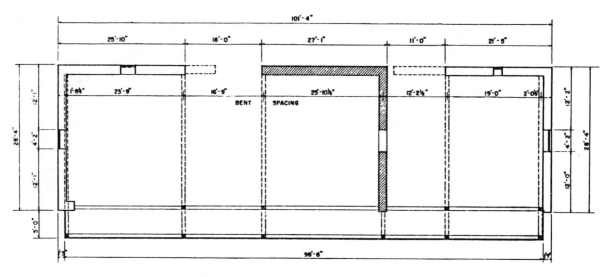

Second-floor plan; this level was used primarily for
storage of hay.

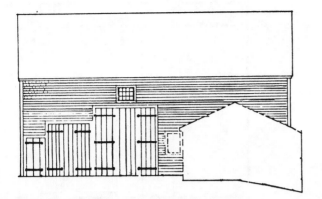

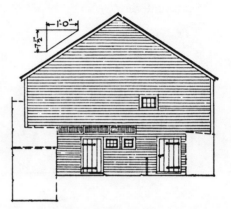

Front and side elevations, barn, Roger Clap property, Dorchester, Mass., 18th century. Because of later additions, this early barn presents an unusual appearance. This was an all-purpose building, containing cow and horse stalls, harness room, milk room, a grain storage area, and a carriage room on the first floor. The second floor was used for storing hay.

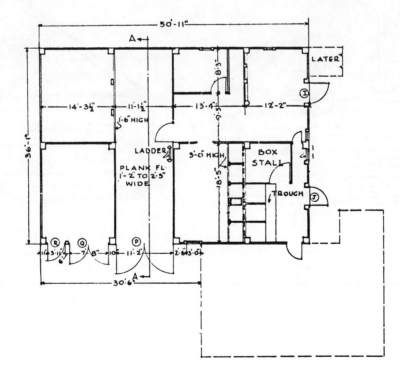

Floor plan.

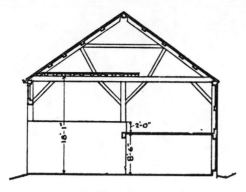

Sectional view.

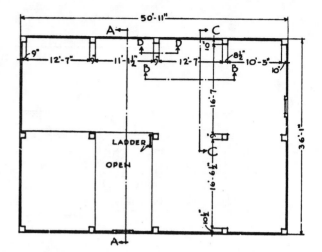

Second-floor plan; this level was reached by means of a ladder.

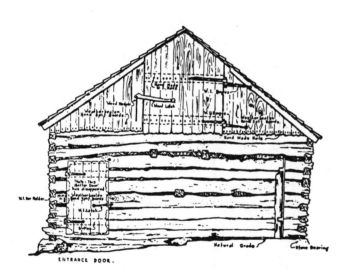

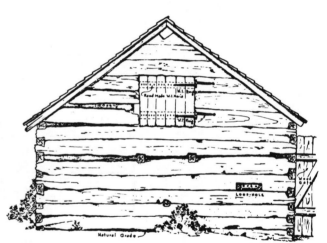

Front elevation, log stable, Stiles farm, Lumberton vicinity, N.J., 17th century. Log barns or stables were once commonplace on the American scene, because they were quickly and cheaply built. Few are extant, however, and everything about this survivor is remarkable. Handmade wrought-iron hardware appears throughout; the logs are, of course, hand-hewn and the boards of the door and the gable are hand-split.

Rear elevation; a small horizontal opening, termed a loophole, is located in the lower right corner. This was used for defense in the days when bellicose Indians still prowled their mid-Atlantic territory.

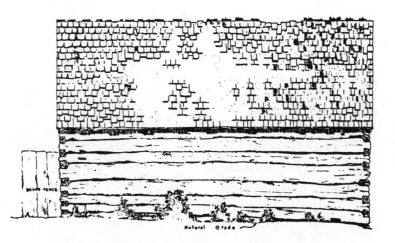

Side elevation; the roofing material is hand-split wood shingles.

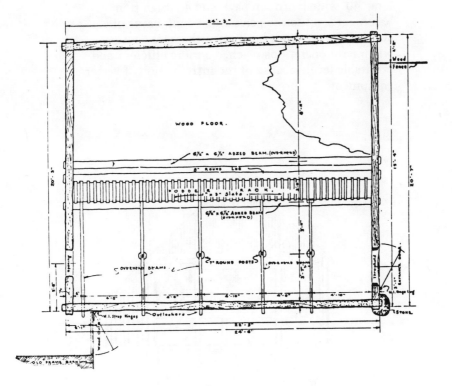

First-floor plan, with five stalls to one side of a center fodder rack.

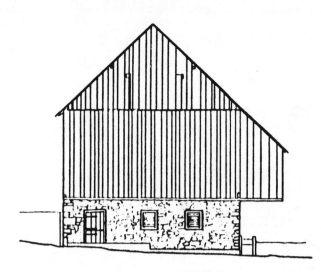

Side elevation.

Side elevation.

Barn, Dundore farm, Mt. Pleasant vicinity, Pa., 1788. A classic Pennsylvania-German bank barn, this frame and stone building is unusually large for such an early date. It measures approximately 125′ long, 40′ wide (with forebay), and 40′ high from basement level to the peak. Most bank barns of a similar size were not built until the next century when farm operations reached a more efficient and profitable level because of the introduction of better equipment.

Sectional view.

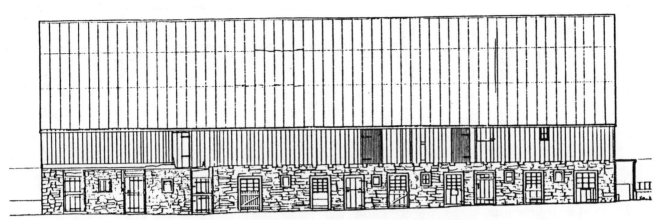

Rear elevation; the forebay extends across the building and provides protection for animals when they are turned out to the barnyard during the day.

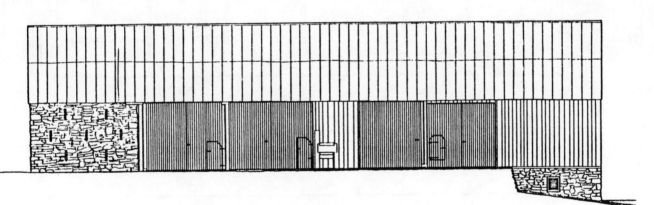

Front elevation; almost the entire length of the building is banked up to provide access to the hay storage areas.

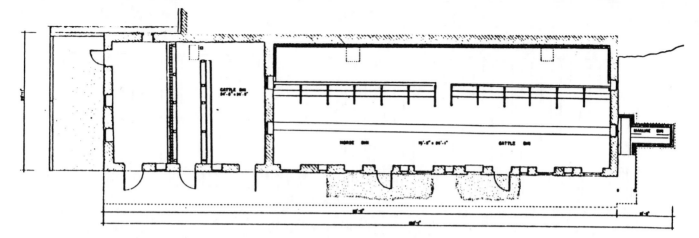

First-floor plan; both cattle and horses were stabled on this level.

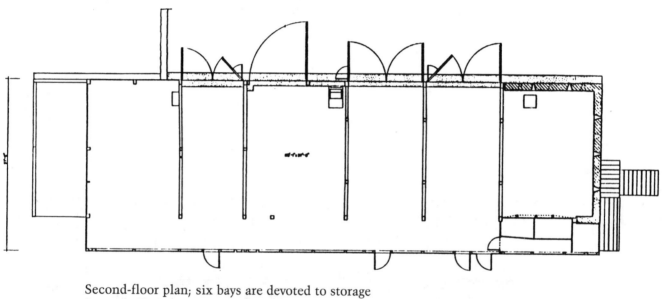

Second-floor plan; six bays are devoted to storage (principally hay) and to threshing.

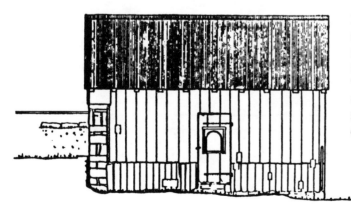

Front elevation, granary, Dundore farm, Mt. Pleasant vicinity, Pa., c. 1840. Grain was probably stored in the large barn previously illustrated before this granary was completed some fifty years later. The first floor was usually given over to threshing equipment and wagons, the precious grain being stored on the second level away from mice and other animals.

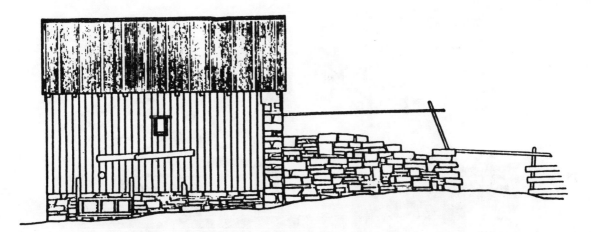

Rear elevation; like other outbuildings on the Dundore farm, the granary is built of wood and random limestone.

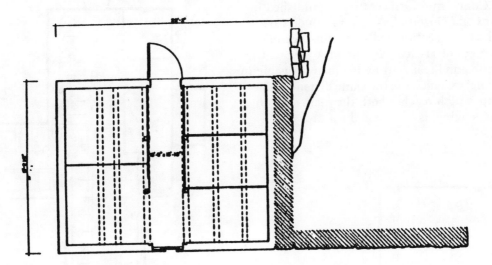

First-floor plan.

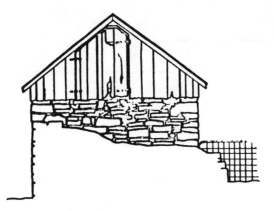

Side elevation.

Rendering, barn, David Lyman farm, Middlefield, Conn., mid-19th century as published in *Barn Plans and Outbuildings* (Orange Judd Co., 1881). The main section and side wing together reach a length of 111 feet, an immense spread; the main section and rear south wing (barely visible in the drawing) extend back the same distance. The split ramp, which reaches both the main section and the side wing, is an unusual feature.

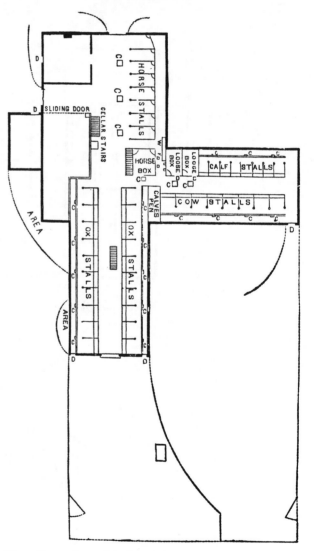

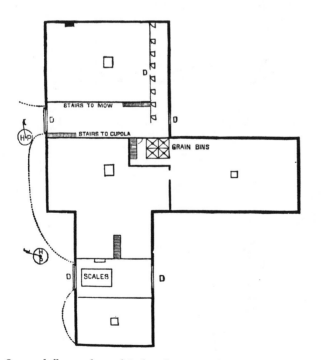

Second-floor plan; this level, accessible via the ramp, was used for hay mows and feed grain bins.

First-floor plan; this level was sometimes termed the "feeding floor," as it contained horse, calf, cow, and ox stalls.

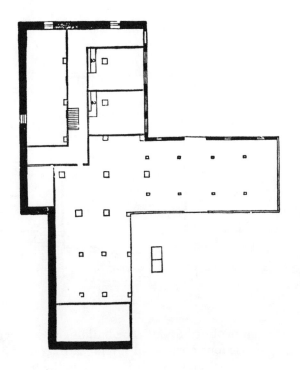

Basement floor plan; the basement level was accessible from the rear of the building and was used for hog pens and the storing of roots and manure.

Rendering and first-floor plan, barn, William B. Collier farm, Audrain County, Mo., mid-19th century, as published in *Barn Plans and Outbuildings* (Orange Judd Co., 1881). Eighty-four feet square, this imposing barn was well designed for housing cattle and horses. The stalls are very generously proportioned, those for horses being nearly six feet wide. Space for wagons and carriages is provided on each side of the central arched entryway. Hay and grain could be lowered easily from the upper level.

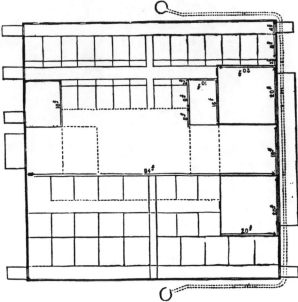

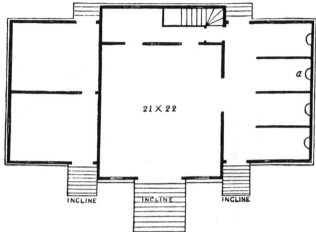

Rendering and first-floor plan, stable, Matthew Vassar estate, Poughkeepsie vicinity, N.Y., as published in *Cottage Residences* by Andrew Jackson Downing (1873). Successful brewer and benefactor Vassar could well afford to build a fashionable stable in what architect Downing termed the "Rustic Pointed Style." The building was designed to house four horses and several carriages as well as a tool house and a workshop. Below the first floor was a basement (not visible) containing a root cellar and room for farm animals.

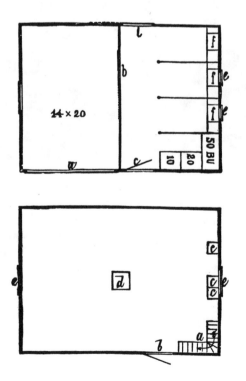

Rendering, first-floor plan and second-floor plan, small barn designed by G. T. Fairchild and published in *Barn Plans and Outbuildings* (Orange Judd Co., 1881). "There are many small farmers, villagers, gardeners, etc.," the designer of this compact building explained, "who wish only barn room enough for a single horse and carriage, and a cow." Fairchild supplied an inexpensive, convenient, and durable design. Grain for feeding was tucked away in bins below the stairway to the loft. Hay and straw could be tossed down the center ventilator, which thus also served as a chute.

Rendering, stable, R. H. Pardee estate, Newburgh vicinity, N.Y., as published in *Cottage Residences* by Andrew Jackson Downing (1873). The hillside brick stable presents a very handsome appearance from the road. Farm equipment, cows, and a manure storage area were well hidden from view in the basement, access to which was from the rear of the building.

Basement floor plan.

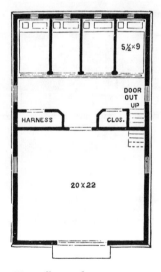

First-floor plan.

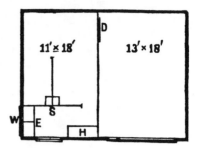

First-floor plan.

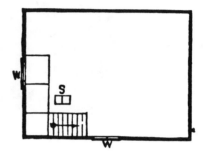

Second-floor plan.

Rendering, barn design from *Barn Plans and Out-buildings* (Orange Judd Co., 1881). A barn such as this was more than adequate for many farm families. It measures 24' long by 18' wide, and there is ample room for several horses and a cow or two as well as a carriage and a farm wagon. The loft, reached by a corner staircase, could hold a good supply of hay and straw.

Front elevation, stable, Worcester, Mass., designed by E. Boyden & Sons, mid-19th century, as published in *Bicknell's Village Builder* by A. J. Bicknell (1872). A horse palace might be a better term for this distinguished brick building. Grain bins were included, but manure and straw for the horses were stored outside in a covered yard. How the second floor was utilized is not known.

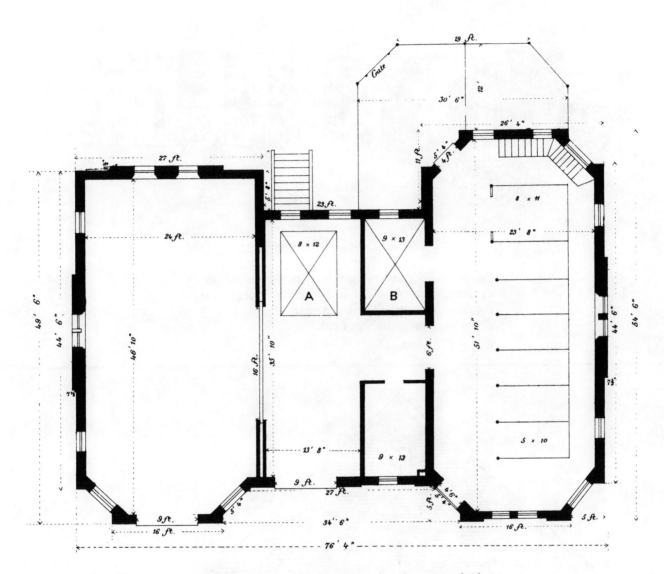

First-floor plan; vehicles entered and were parked at left and horses were stabled to the right. The center section contained a harness room and compartments for washing carriages and horses. Unlike many stables, this building was extremely well lighted and ventilated.

Rendering; the exceptional attention lavished on each architectural element is clearly evident in this romantic vignette. The main entrance and loft doors were presumably of oak.

Front elevation, barn, built by John H. Dewitt, Wallpack Center vicinity, N.J., early 19th century. With gable-end doors, the Dewitt barn shows the influence of the Dutch barn-building tradition in early America. The steeply pitched roof and high hay loft are also characteristic of many barns found in sections of New York and New Jersey settled by the Dutch.

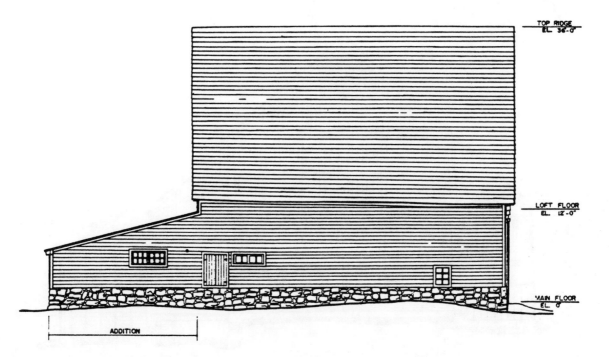

TOP RIDGE
EL 36'-0"

LOFT FLOOR
EL 12'-0"

MAIN FLOOR
EL 0'

ADDITION

Side elevation; the extraordinary pitch and extent of the roof are visibly evident.

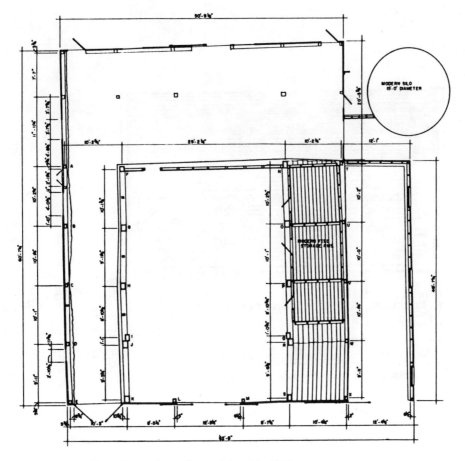

MODERN SILO
15'-0" DIAMETER

First-floor plan; the original building measures approximately 40' square and is flanked by two additions.

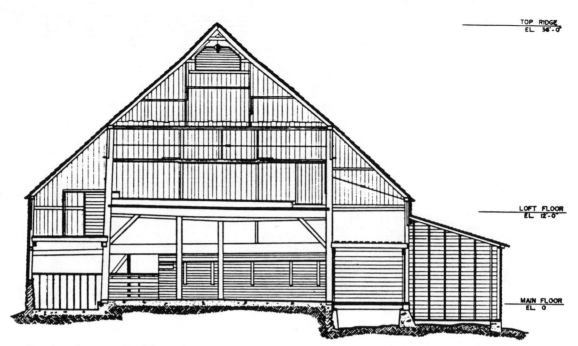

TOP RIDGE
EL 36'-0"

LOFT FLOOR
EL 12'-0"

MAIN FLOOR
EL 0

Sectional view of gable end.

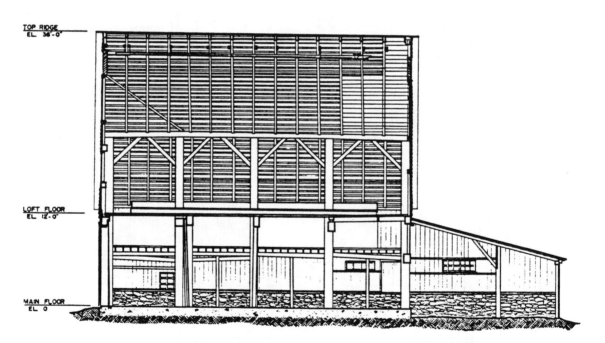

TOP RIDGE
EL 36'-0"

LOFT FLOOR
EL 12'-0"

MAIN FLOOR
EL 0

Sectional view from side with rear addition.

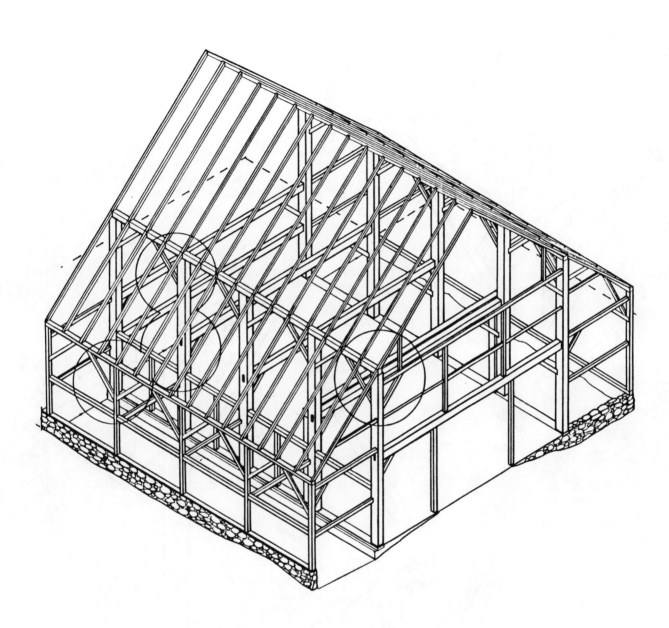

Isometric drawing of structural framing; all timbers
are hand-hewn.

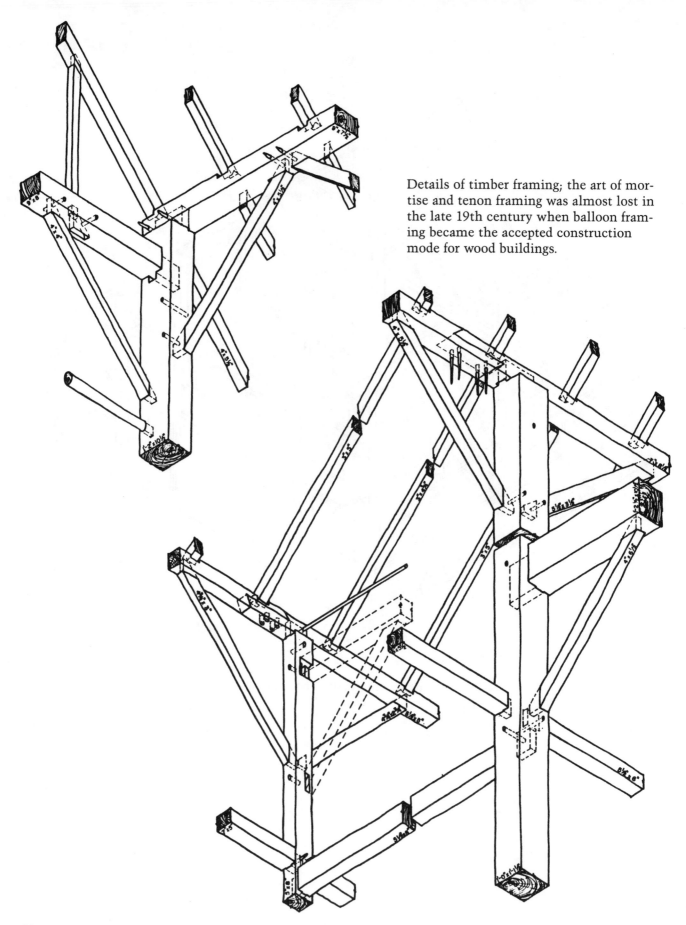

Details of timber framing; the art of mortise and tenon framing was almost lost in the late 19th century when balloon framing became the accepted construction mode for wood buildings.

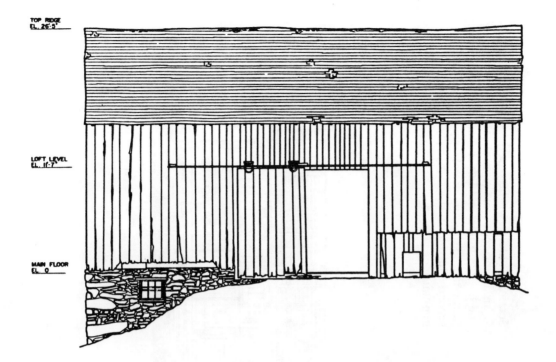

Front and rear elevations, barn, Walter-Kautz farm, Shawnee on Delaware, Pa., early 19th century. Set on a stone foundation, the frame barn has three main levels and is built into a hillside. The sliding doors of the front ramp entrance are a characteristic 19th-century feature. The rear elevation shows the shed addition; in form it is a forebay supported by pillars.

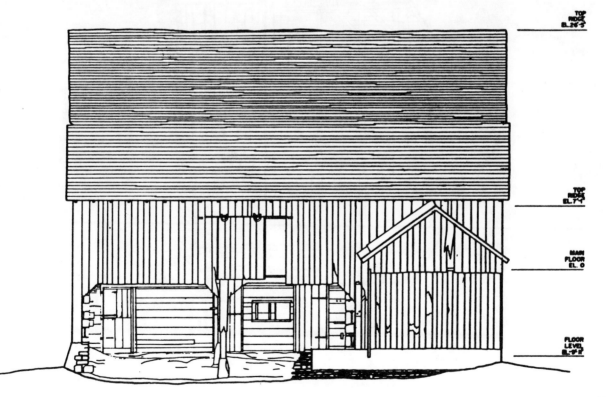

Sectional side view; the basement level for small animals and root storage, main floor for threshing and large animals, and loft for hay and straw storage in the main structure are clearly delineated. The second addition to the right may have served as a henhouse or piggery.

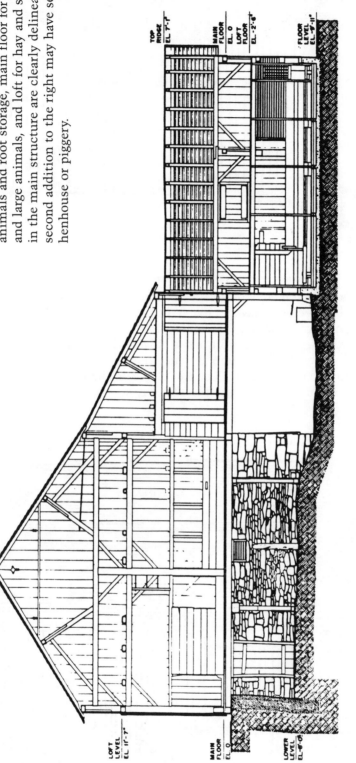

Side elevation; when drawn, the barn was in poor condition, much of the siding having deteriorated. The building appears always to have been poorly ventilated as there is little evidence of windows or other means for circulating light and air.

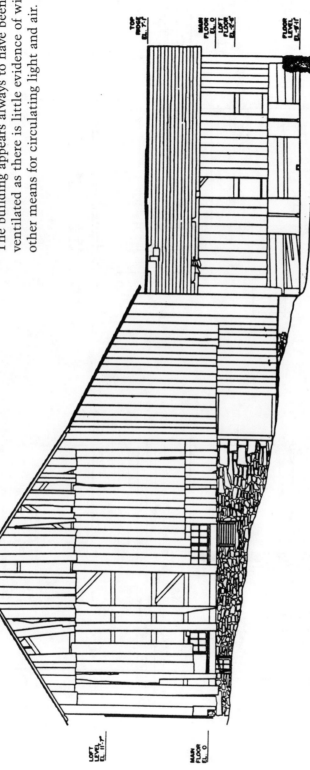

TOP RIDGE EL. 21'-1"

MAIN FLOOR EL. 0

LOFT FLOOR EL. 3'-4"

FLOOR LEVEL EL. -4'-11"

LOFT LEVEL EL. 11'-7"

MAIN FLOOR EL. 0

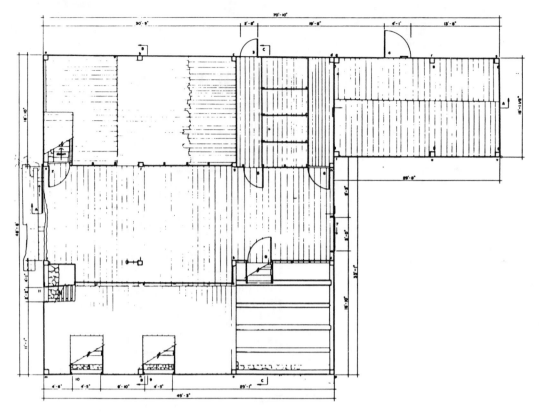

First-floor plan.

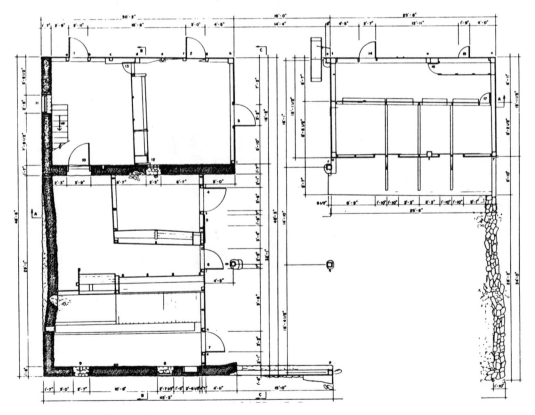

Basement floor plan.

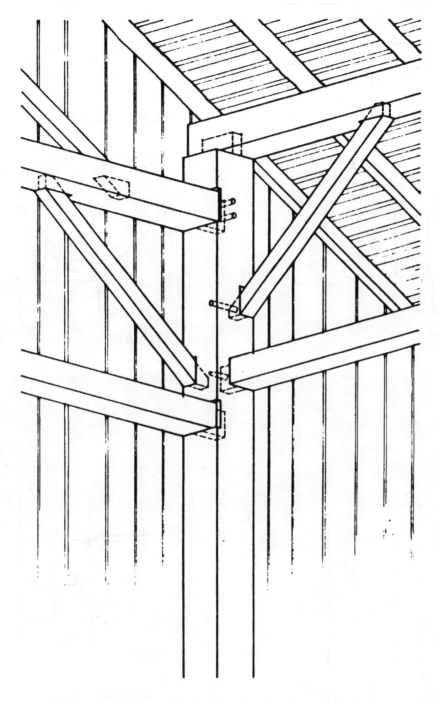

Construction details of timber framing in original
main structure.

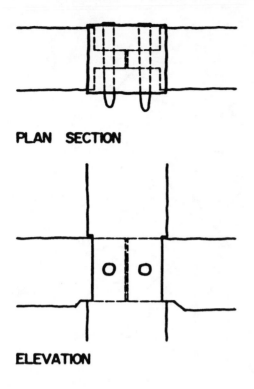

PLAN SECTION

ELEVATION

Elevation and sectional plan of connection.

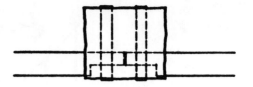

PLAN SECTION

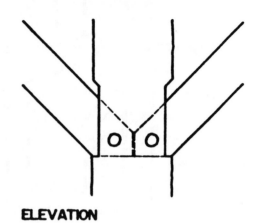

ELEVATION

Elevation and sectional plan of connection.

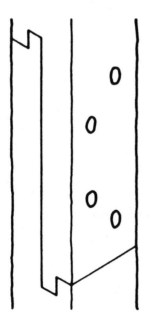

Column splice.

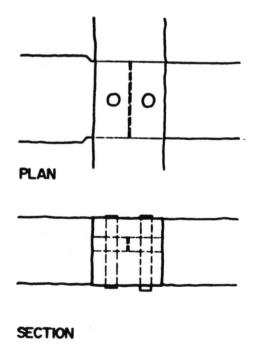

PLAN

SECTION

Elevation and sectional plan of connection.

Side elevation, barn, Joseph Conrad farm, Mt. Pleasant vicinity, Pa., c. 1850, with later addition c. 1880. Rental of the side of a barn for commercial advertising became a common practice in the 20th century. Today, now that much of the lettering has faded away to a soft blur, such decoration is considered nostalgic and picturesque. The Irvindale bungalow plots were located on the farm property and the development was one of several commercial enterprises, including a grist mill and warehouse, undertaken by the owners.

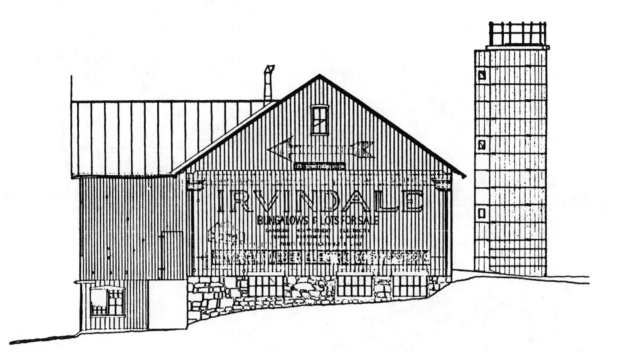

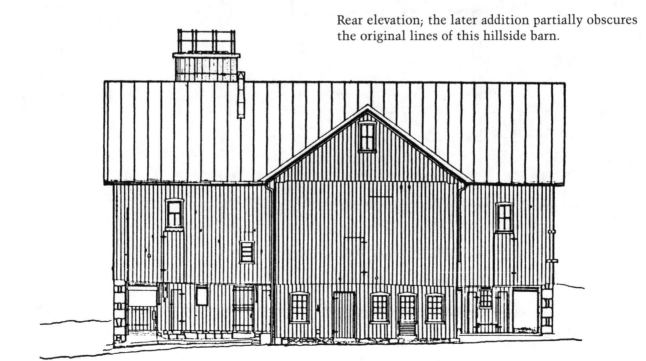

Rear elevation; the later addition partially obscures the original lines of this hillside barn.

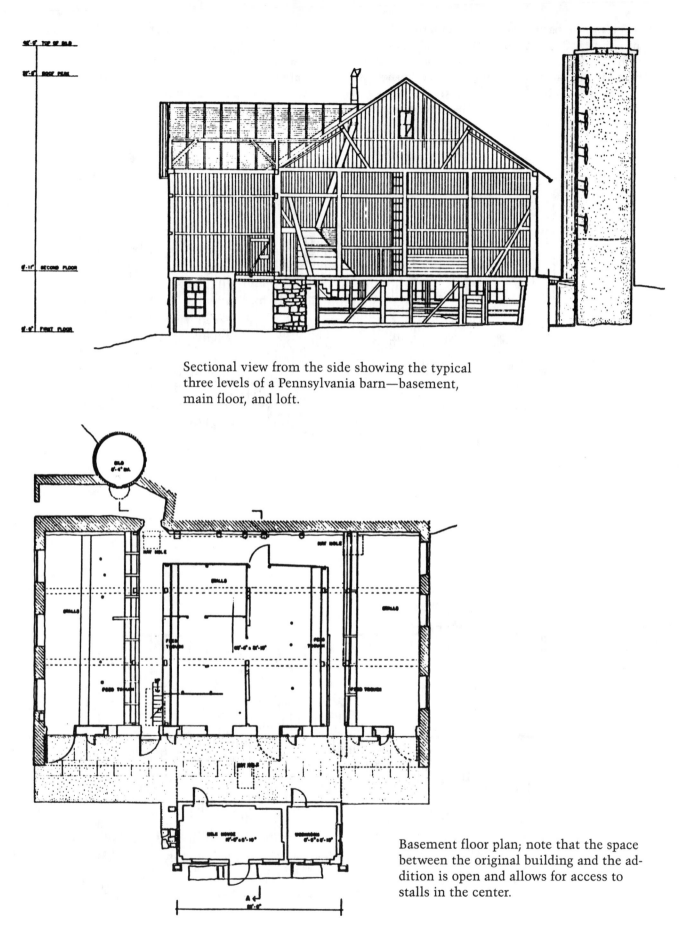

Sectional view from the side showing the typical three levels of a Pennsylvania barn—basement, main floor, and loft.

Basement floor plan; note that the space between the original building and the addition is open and allows for access to stalls in the center.

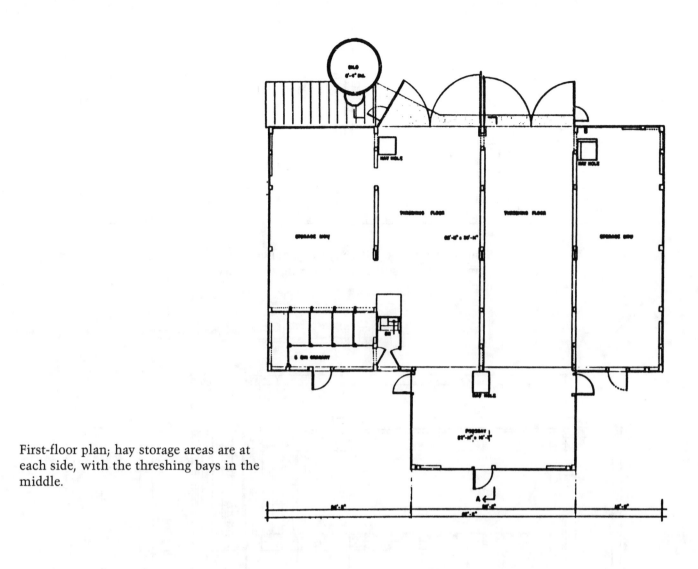

First-floor plan; hay storage areas are at each side, with the threshing bays in the middle.

Front elevation, barn, Reynolds-Gentry ranch, Albany vicinity, Tex., late 1870s. This handsome barn has now been relocated to the Ranching Heritage Center, Texas Tech University, in Lubbock.

George T. Reynolds built the barn of pine brought in by train from the Dallas area. The building was later used by Mart B. Gentry to house his thoroughbred horses.

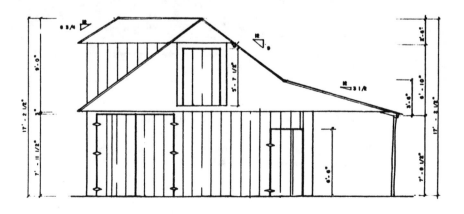

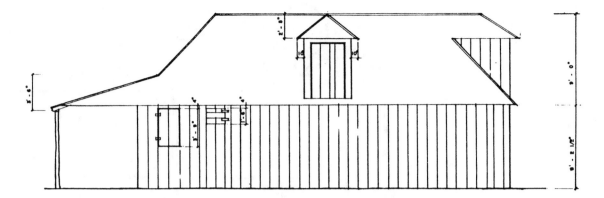

Side elevation; the loft level was smaller than in
many barns but sufficent for storing a quantity of
hay.

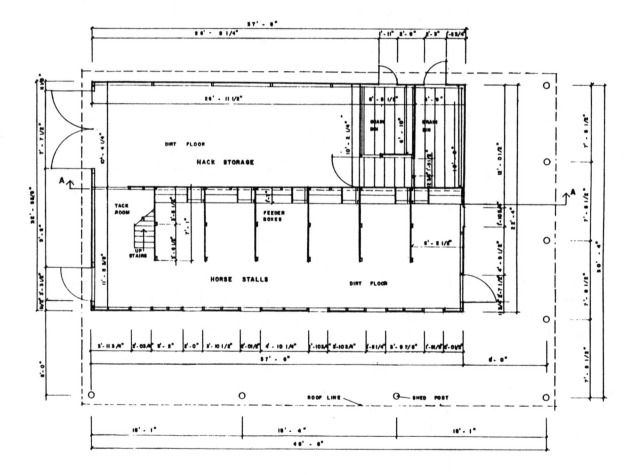

First-floor plan; grain bins were found in the upper
right corner, and each was equipped with a chute to
dispense corn and feed to the feeder boxes which
ran along the center of the floor.

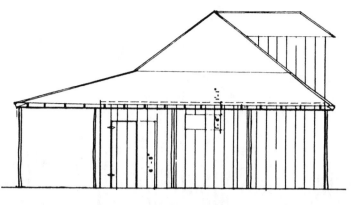

Rear elevation.

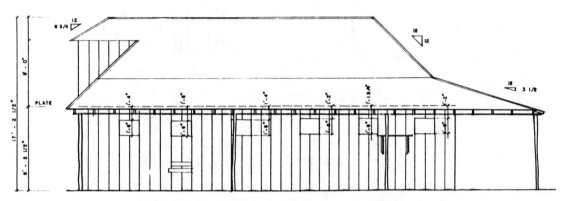

Side elevation; the horse stalls were well lit and
ventilated by a series of small windows below the
eaves.

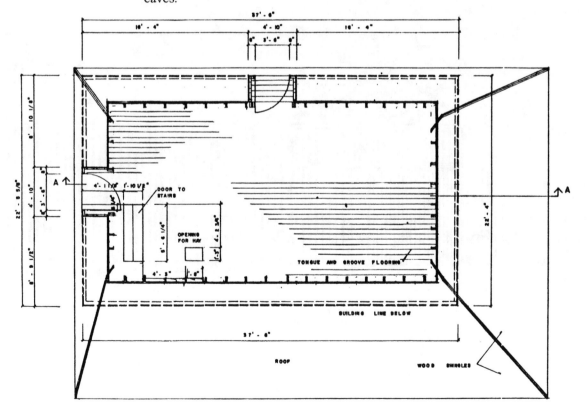

Second-floor plan.

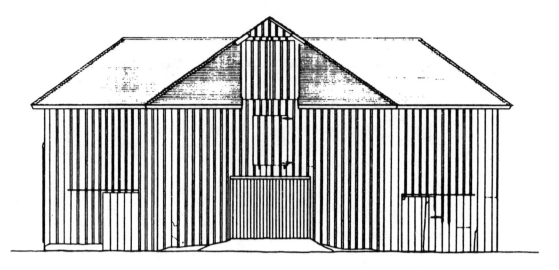

Front elevation, barn, Laguna Seco Rancho, Coyote vicinity, Calif., 1840s. This central building served a large grain and stock operation begun by William Fisher and successfully enlarged by his son Fiacro.

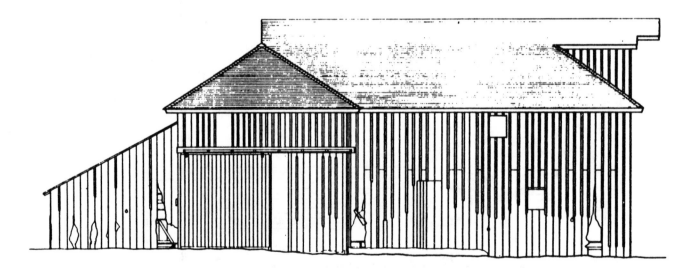

Side elevation showing two additions.

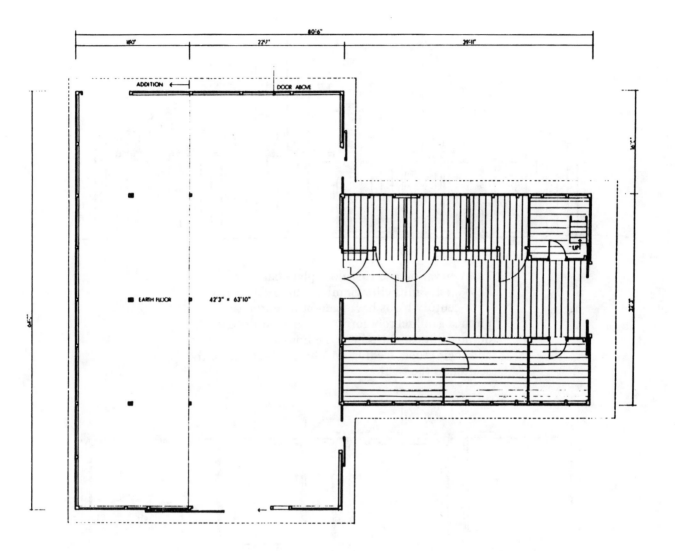

First-floor plan containing stalls in the front and a
large (42'3" by 63'10") area for other operations.

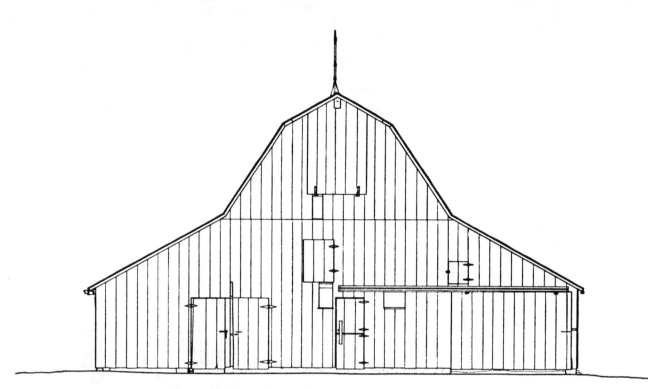

Front elevation and first-floor plan, barn, Reuben
Ross farm, Smithville vicinity, Mo., 1925. Many
20th-century barns have been built in the tri-
pitched gambrel roof form. The ground-floor level is
devoted almost entirely to the housing of animals
and their proper feeding. Machinery is stored in the
section to the right.

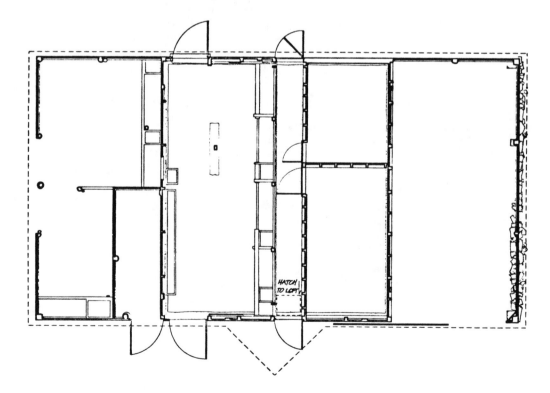

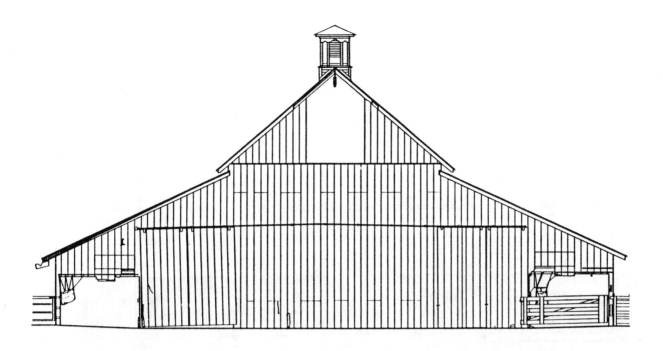

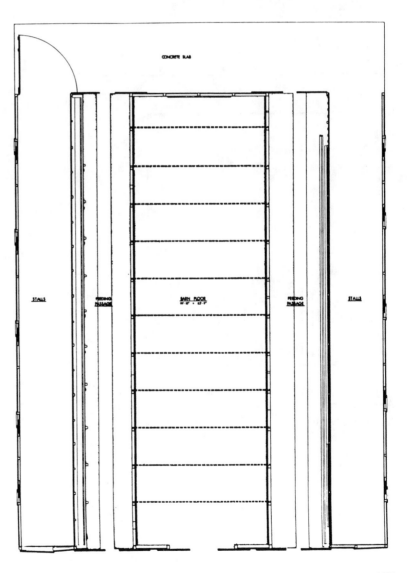

Front elevation and first-floor plan, cow barn, Eschenburg-Silva farm, Gilroy, Calif., 1880s. Dairy barns of this period in central California frequently follow these lines—a central bay flanked by low shed-roofed wings. In the center was the main dairy floor and the feeding passages; the cow stalls lined each side.

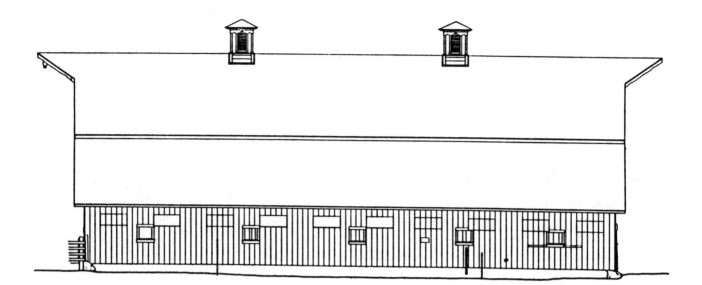

Side elevation; note the use of two cupola ventilators.

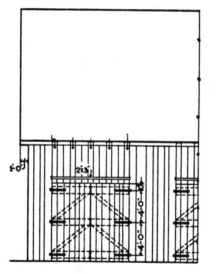

Elevation of typical south bay, tobacco barn, Agawam, Mass., 19th century. The air curing of tobacco requires special conditions, ventilation being primary. This Connecticut Valley barn is divided into twelve bays, each being either 5'7'' or 5'10'' wide.

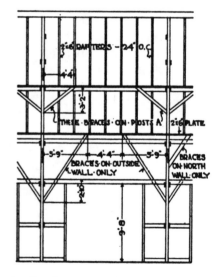

Longitudinal section of typical south bay.

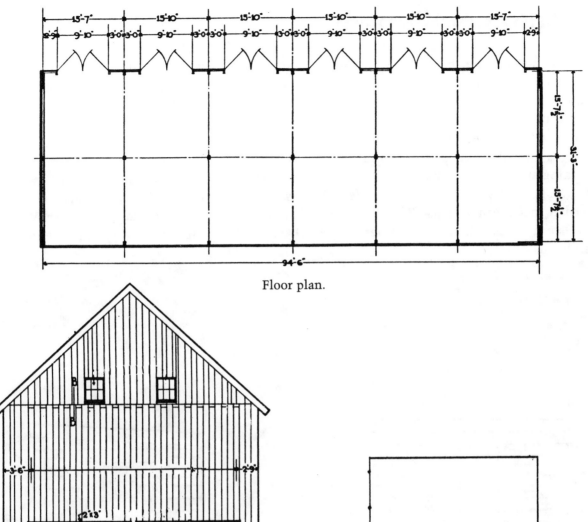

Floor plan.

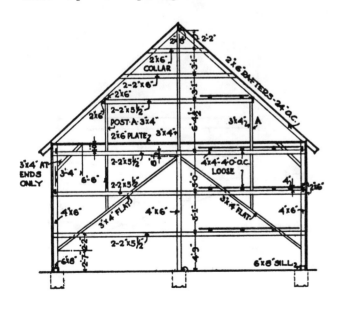

Elevation of typical north bay; seven of the boards are vents which are sprung out and propped into place to be held open when tobacco is being air cured—a process requiring three to twelve weeks.

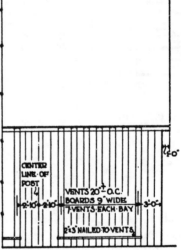

Elevation of gable end and cross-section of gable-end framing; tobacco is air cured by hanging the cords of leaves on sticks which are then arranged on the barn's tier poles.

10. Summer Kitchens

A separate building for the preparation and cooking of food may be the oldest structure found on an 18th- or early 19th-century farm. Usually modestly proportioned, the summer kitchen might have served as a dwelling place until a more substantial residence could be built to house a growing family. When no longer needed for its original purpose, the building was converted to another practical use. And practical it was during the warmer months of the year, when it was best to prepare food in as cool and well ventilated a location as possible. The summerhouse was also often used for such fair weather activities as canning and preserving foods. The building was sparsely furnished, perhaps holding a work table, dining table, chairs and benches, and a few shelves. Many summer kitchens, of course, were built at a later date than the main house. This is especially true on a majority of large mid-19th century Midwestern and Western farms, where the summer kitchen also served as a dining hall for the numerous farm or ranch hands.

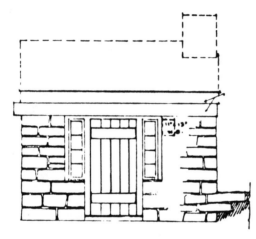

Front elevation.

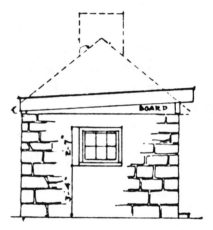

Side elevation.

Summer kitchen, Israel Swayze farm, Hope vicinity, N.J., 18th century. Known as the "outside kitchen," the stone building was a simple 10'3" by 13'4" rectangle set into a steep hillside. It was built for cooking and baking, the cooking activity being transferred to the newer building seen in the floor plan on the opposite page. The little building is distinguished by the use of sidelights at the entranceway.

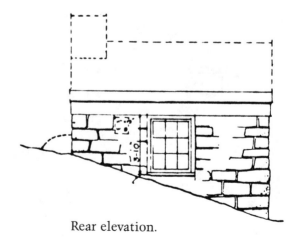

Rear elevation.

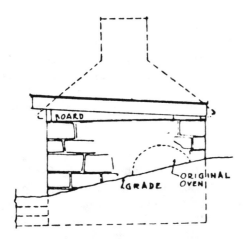

Side elevation.

Sectional view.

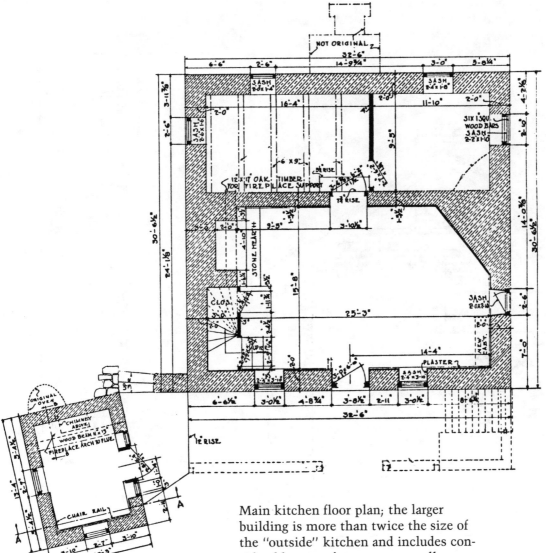

Main kitchen floor plan; the larger building is more than twice the size of the "outside" kitchen and includes considerable space for storage as well as cooking.

Floor plan.

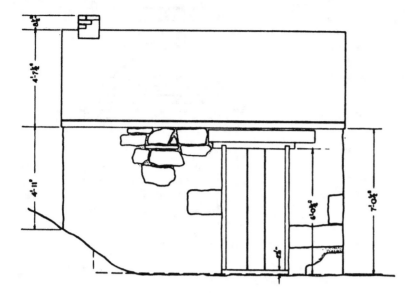

Summer kitchen, John H. Vreeland property, Towaco, N.J., 18th century. The Vreeland building is approximately the same size as the first Swayze kitchen and just as simple in construction and plan. Between its solid 1½'-thick fieldstone walls were only a cooking fireplace and Dutch oven. The position of the wrought-iron crane for hanging pots over the fire is evident; iron bars for hanging hams and other meats are in place several feet above it.

Front elevation.

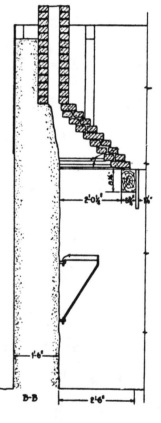

Sectional view of fireplace and flue.

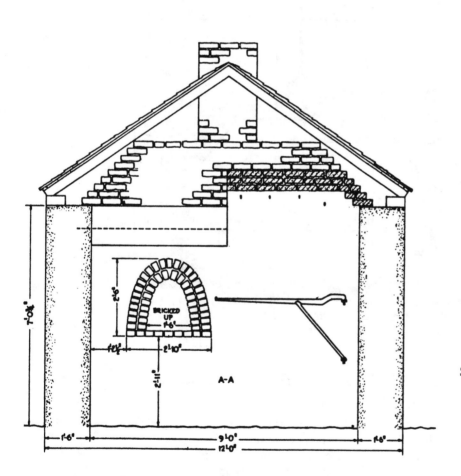

Sectional view of gable end.

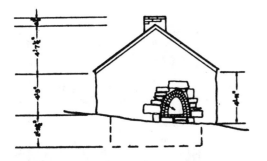

Side elevation, showing position of Dutch oven.

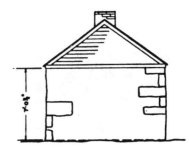

Side elevation.

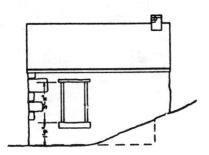

Rear elevation.

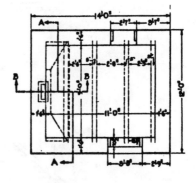

Floor plan.

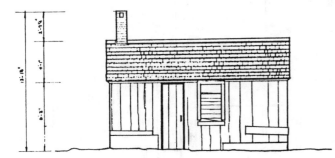

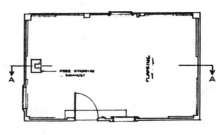

Floor plan.

Front elevation, summer kitchen, Elisha Cobb farm, Truro vicinity, Mass., mid-19th century. A little over 17' long and 10' wide, this ramshackle building has barely survived the elements. Everything about the structure except its floor plan is random, including the siding and flooring. A freestanding cookstove was positioned at one gable end.

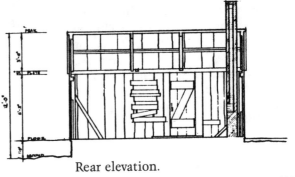

Rear elevation.

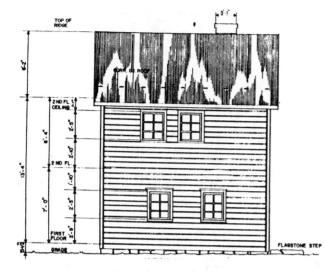

Side elevation.

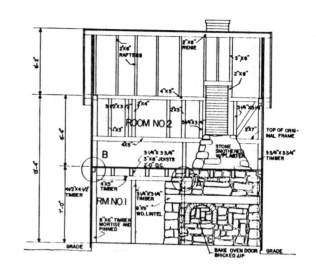

Side sectional view.

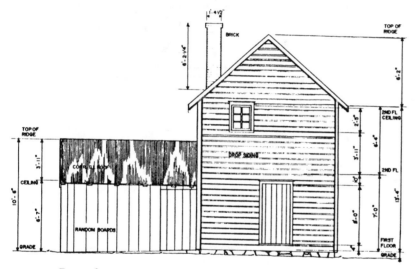

Rear elevation.

Summer kitchen, Snyder property, Gettysburg vicinity, Pa., early 19th century; later addition, c. 1890. The development from a small one-and-a-half story kitchen to a full two-story building with a woodshed addition can be traced in these drawings and those on the following page. The upper portion of the chimney is of brick and is an obvious extension of the lower stone stack; a bake oven was originally located in the fireplace wall and has been bricked up. The oven protruded into the space now occupied by the woodshed.

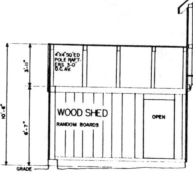
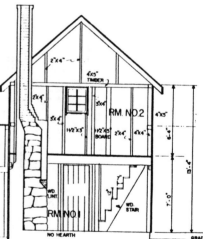

Rear sectional view.

112

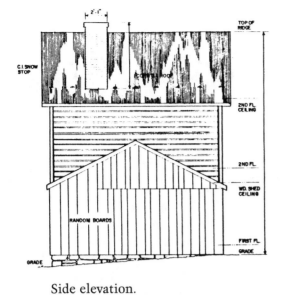

Side elevation.

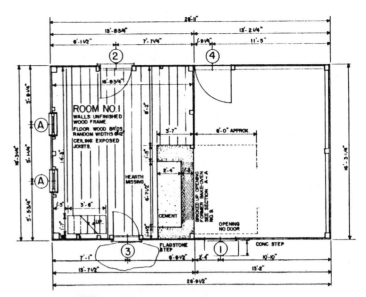

First-floor plan; a stone floor underlies part of the earth floor of the shed, this earlier base extending outward from the bake oven extension.

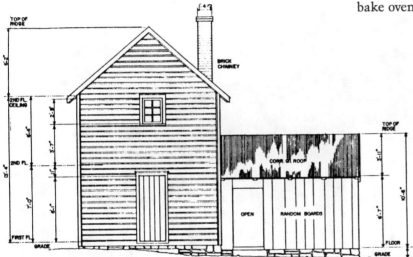

Front elevation.

Second-floor plan; the room is only framed out and not finished. It may have served as a storeroom or sleeping quarters for a cook or other hired hand.

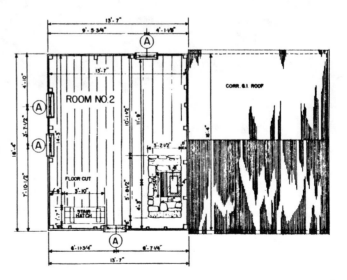

11. Tool Houses

Separate houses for storing tools were not commonly built on the early American farm, as the wagon shed or carriage house sufficed for storage in most situations. But when there was a special need for housing a large collection of tools, such as those required by a blacksmith, a separate building was constructed. It was likely, however, to be a dual purpose structure. Later in the mid-19th century, fancy building designs for tool houses were recommended by writers in the agricultural papers and authors of house-plan books. Those who followed the advice were principally gentleman farmers and estate owners who were interested as much in the architecturally picturesque as the practical. It did, however, make as much sense then to have a separate place to store garden tools as it does today.

Rendering, tool house, Townsend Sharpless summer residence, Birmingham Township, Chester County, Pa., as published in *The American Agriculturist* (1862). Measuring 20' long by 12' wide, this tool house was a temple of order and precision. Such examples were rare in 19th-century rural America.

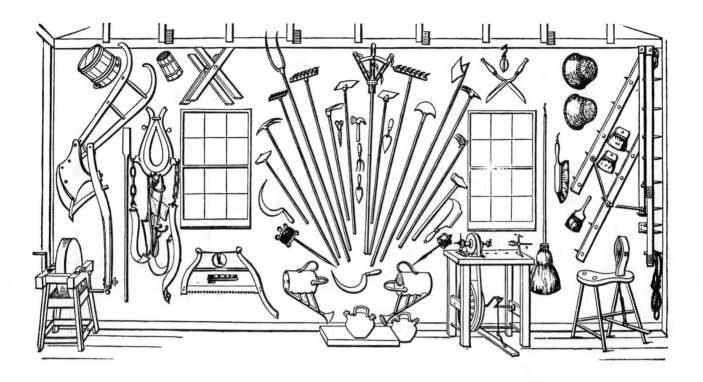

Interior views of the tool house. The article on the Sharpless outbuilding was accompanied by a homily in verse: "All ranged in order, and disposed with grace/Shape marked of each, and each one in its place;/Nor this alone the curious eye to please,/But to be found, whene'er required with ease./If used or loaned, and not returned by rule,/The vacant shape will show the missing tool;/Thus often urged the careless will improve,/And rules of order soon will learn to love."

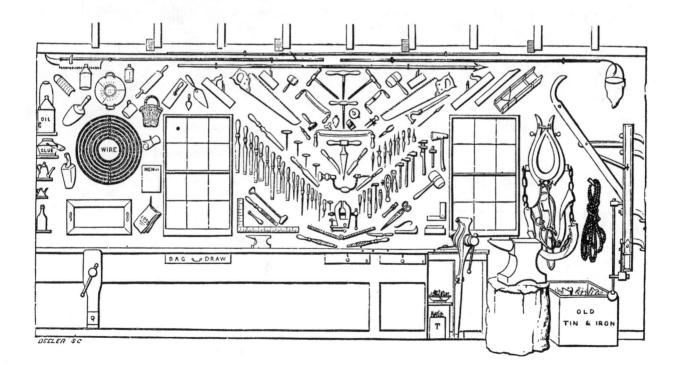

Rendering and floor plan, combination toolshed and privy, published in *Villas and Cottages* by Calvert Vaux (1864). The fashion for rustic and picturesque outbuildings was in full favor by the mid-century. The Vaux design called for rough bark-covered siding, corner posts, and trim.

Front elevation.

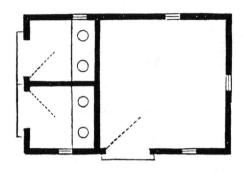

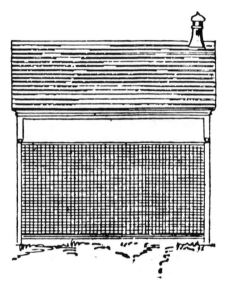

Side elevation.

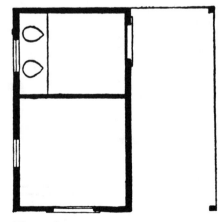

Floor plan.

Combination tool house and privy, published in *Palliser's New Cottage Homes and Details* (Palliser, Palliser & Co., 1887). With its shingled gable and paneled walls, this multi-purpose building displays aspects of the then popular Queen Anne style.

12. Well Houses

The well house or pump house, as it was later known, served primarily to shelter a hand-dug well from the elements. The structure had to be open enough to allow access to the wellhead, but sufficiently enclosed to prevent animals or humans from falling down the watery abyss. Such wells, usually stone-lined, had an average depth of 25' to 30'. The early well house also provided a framework for affixing a mechanism such as a winch and pulley with which to bring up pails of water. Pumps for the same purpose became common in the 19th century, and the shelter served to protect these valuable devices. Latticework pump buildings, housing hand pumps and modern electric or gas-driven devices, can still be seen in rural areas.

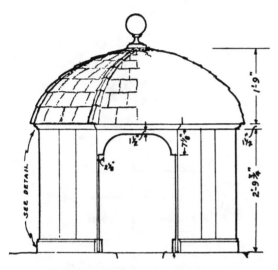

Front elevation.

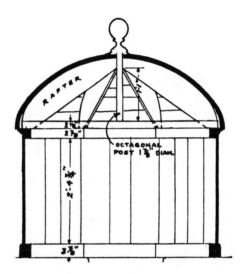

Sectional view.

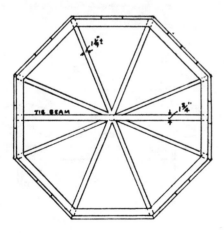

Roof framing plan.

Well house, Gov. Jonathan Belcher Place, Milton, Mass., late 18th century. The graceful shelter was built to protect a well fed by the "Old Indian Spring." The floor was of stone pavers; the roof, of wood shingles. The wood siding and trim were painted red to match the color of the main house.

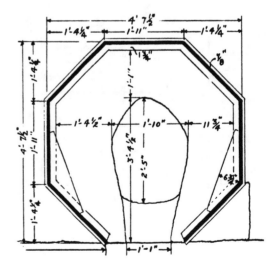

Floor plan.

117

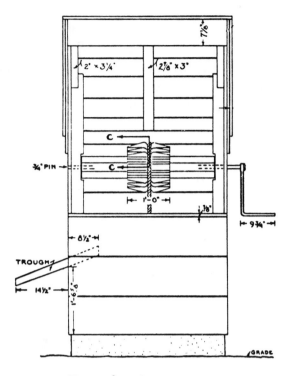

Front elevation.

Well house, Squire William Sever property, Kingston, Mass., late 18th century. A windlass and rope pulley were used to lower and raise a bucket. The wrought-iron crank for turning the mechanism is shown at one side of the cut-away structure. The well house was painted yellow to match the color of the main house, had a wood-shingled roof, and was sided with tongue-and-groove boards.

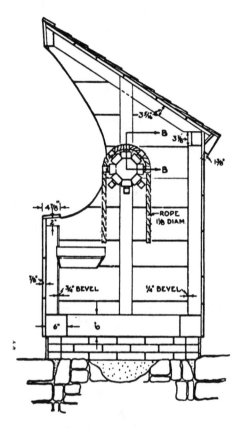

Side elevation.

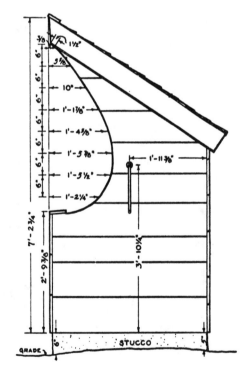

Side elevation.

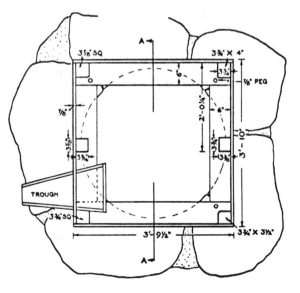

Floor plan.

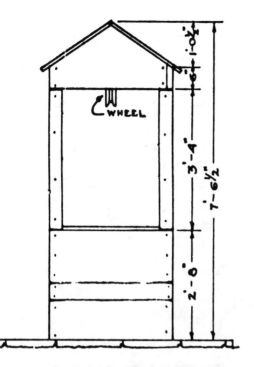

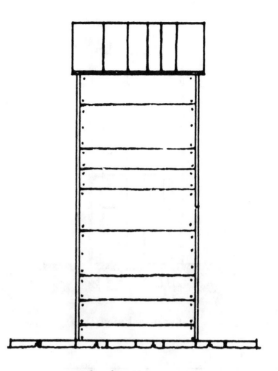

Front elevation, well house, Robert Manning Place, Salem, Mass., 1825. The simple shelter provides protection for the well and a mechanism for drawing water. The wheel is threaded through a wood axle in the upper section.

Side elevation.

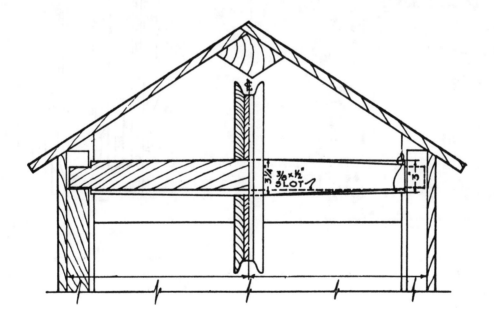

Sectional view of wheel mounting.

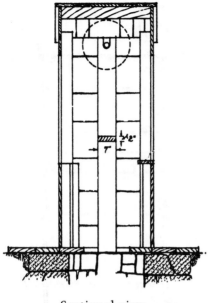

Sectional view.

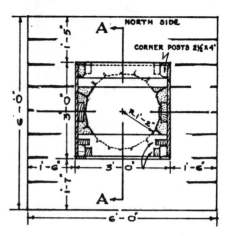

Floor plan; the 3'-square area surrounding the wellhead is stone-paved and stone coping surrounds the opening.

Elevation, well-house design published in *Home Building* by E. C. Hussey (1876). With its gingerbread cornice, bargeboards and decorative incised panels, this building was appropriate for a country or village property. The wellhead projects several feet from the ground. Undoubtedly, the shelter was intended to be fitted with a pump and a trough to carry away the overflow.

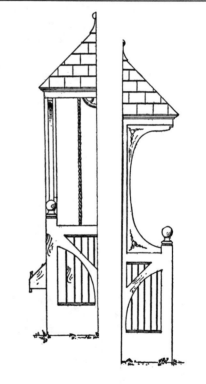

Half-elevation from the front and half-elevation from the side, well-house design published in *Palliser's New Cottage Homes and Details* (Palliser, Palliser & Co., 1887). The frame of this well house is cut away on two sides to give access to the well. A wheel mechanism is used for lowering and raising a pail. Presumably, this well was utilized for occasional rather than daily use.

13. Woodhouses and Woodsheds

The most common shelter for wood was attached in the form of a lean-to to another building such as the main house, a smokehouse, or the barn. On large farms and estates, however, a separate outbuilding was frequently built for wood storage. Most of these buildings were primitive sheds open on at least one side away from the prevailing winds. Another simple shelter might be located on the edge of the wood lot some distance away from the main farm buildings to serve as a way station. More sophisticated woodhouses were built on some gentlemanly estates where every outbuilding, however lowly its purpose, was considered worthy of aesthetic attention.

Elevation of front as it exists today, woodhouse, Edmund Freeman farm, Truro, Mass., 19th century. Although a small building—with a later wing—the woodhouse extends one-and-a-half stories and may have been used originally for other purposes. How it must have appeared when first built is suggested in the drawing to the right.

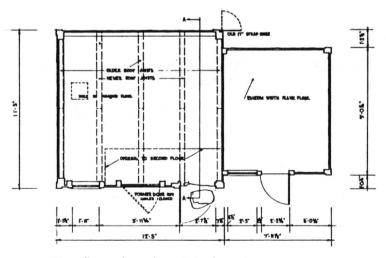

First-floor plan; the original section measures approximately 12′ square.

Front and rear elevations, woodshed, Adams National Historic Site, Quincy, Mass., early 19th century. Despite the shed roof, the Adams building is considerably more sophisticated than most such buildings. The graceful arches and door heads are stylistic touches of the Federal period.

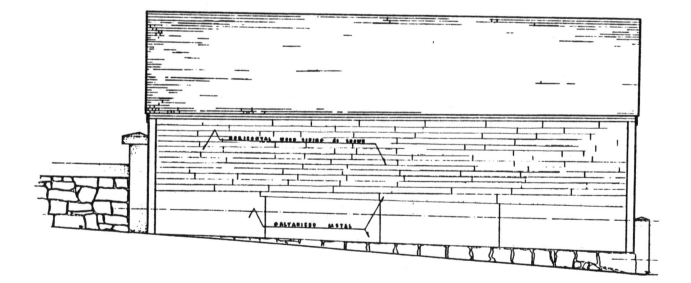

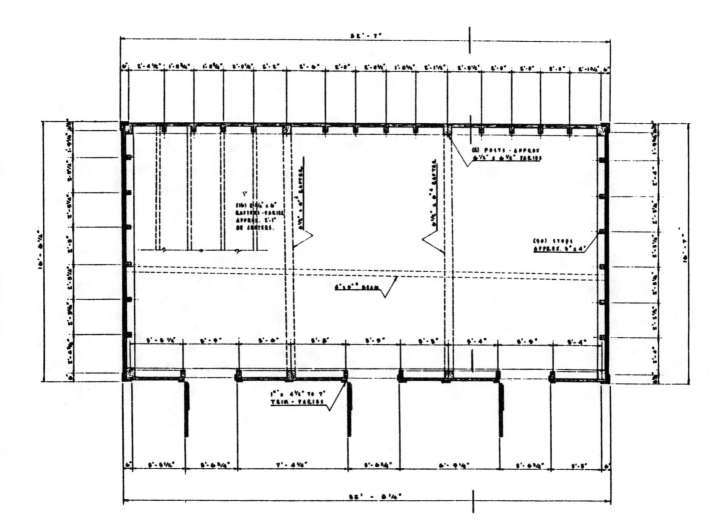

Floor plan; the building is divided into three storage
bays, each with its own entrance. As is true of most
woodsheds, there are no windows.

Selected Reading

PRIMARY SOURCES

Architectural style books of the 19th century provide much useful information on the types of building plans which were available to the prosperous working farmer or gentleman farmer. For the most part, these volumes are what one terms "high style"; that is, the contents are devoted as much to aesthetic considerations as to the practical needs of the farmer. Another type of book, better called a building manual rather than a style book, was addressed to the concerns of the common farmer. Many of the plans included in this type of anthology were drawn from farm journals and newspapers.

Allen, Lewis F. *Rural Architecture.* New York: C. M. Saxton, 1852.

Published in six editions from 1852 to 1865, this is an important source of 19th-century farmhouse and outbuilding plans. Of more practical use to the average country dweller than the works of Downing or Vaux, Lewis's book was extremely popular and as concerned with pigpens as carriage houses. *Rural Architecture* may be found today in some large public library collections and in rare book shops.

Downing, Andrew Jackson. *The Architecture of Country Houses.* Reprint of the 1850 edition. New York: Dover Publications, 1969.

The best-known of American architectural books set aesthetic standards which would guide country gentlemen for generations. Downing's theories of "Picturesque Architecture" had an influence on many fellow architects. This work was, in part, an American version of an earlier and very popular English volume, the *Encyclopedia of Cottage, Farm, and Villa Architecture and Furniture*, by J. C. Loudoun.

Downing, Andrew Jackson. *Cottage Residences.* 1873 edition reprinted as *Victorian Cottage Residences.* New York: Dover Publications, 1981.

First published in 1842, Downing's first book is primarily a collection of country house plans. Little attention is devoted to the needs of the working farmer. The book, however, provides a remarkable view of what could be done to beautify a country house.

Halsted, Bryan D., ed. *Barn Plans and Outbuildings.* 1881 edition reprinted as *Barns, Sheds, and Outbuildings.* Brattleboro, Vt.: The Stephen Greene Press, 1977.

Practical in every respect, this work compiled by Halsted for the Orange Judd publishing company brings together many of the building projects first introduced in Judd's periodical, *The American Agriculturist.*

Vaux, Calvert. *Villas and Cottages.* Reprint of the second edition, 1864. New York: Dover Publications, 1970.

Vaux was briefly—from 1850 to 1852—Downing's partner, and he shared a love for the picturesque in building style. The designs shown in this volume are even more elaborate than those executed or endorsed by Downing. Among the special features of the book are the vignettes and details of small outbuildings and garden structures, some in the rustic style.

Woodward, George E. *Woodward's Architecture and Rural Art.* One-volume reprint of vols. I and II, 1867 and 1868. Watkins Glen, N.Y.: American Life Foundation, 1978.

A wide variety of farm houses, cottages, and outbuildings are included in this compilation of plans. The designs in volume I are quite modest in scope but are appealingly ornamental. There are designs for icehouses, wellhouses, and toolsheds in addition to those for barns and stables.

SECONDARY SOURCES

The number of books which survey period country architecture, particularly outbuildings and barns, is extremely limited. County and regional histories of rural areas may prove to be excellent sources of illustrations for anyone rebuilding, building anew, or simply studying barns and other types of structures.

Arthur, Eric, and Dudley Witney. *The Barn: A Vanishing Landmark in North America.* Boston: New York Graphic Society, 1972.

A pictorial survey of Canadian and some American barn types in the Northeast.

Grow, Lawrence. *The Old House Book of Outdoor Living Spaces.* New York: Warner Books, 1981.

An illustrated history of outdoor structures in rural and urban areas with special attention given to porches, verandas, and garden buildings.

Long, Amos. *The Pennsylvania German Farm.* Publications of The Pennsylvania German Society, vol. VI. Breinigsville, Pa.: The Pennsylvania German Society, 1972.

Authoritative and detailed, this is the finest regional study of farm architecture available. It is a particularly useful source of information on the development of the Pennsylvania bank or hillside barn. The book contains hundreds of informative photographs, and many of the building types shown can be found in other regions as well.

Rawson, Richard. *Old Barn Plans.* New York: Bonanza Books, 1982.

A compilation of elevations, floor plans, and details of six North American barn types—primitive barns, early English and Dutch barns, bank barns, experimental barns, Victorian barns, and modern barns.

Strombeck, Janet A. and Richard H. *Backyard Structures: Designs & Plans.* Delafield, Wis.: Sun Designs, 1982.

Adaptations of traditional designs for modern use. Included are storage sheds, cabanas, garbage can enclosures, studios, doghouses, and small barns.